ECHOES OF FATE

From Birth To The Last Heartbeats

Assim Salih

Copyright 2024 A. Salih
ISBN: 979-8-218-42119-9
First edition: April 2024

The authors have asserted their moral right under the Copyright, Designs and Patents Act 1988, to be identified as the author of work.

All rights reserved. No parts of this publication may be reproduced, copied, stored in a retrieval system, or transmitted, in any form by any means without the prior written consent of the copy holder, nor be otherwise circulated in any form of binding or other than that in which it is published and without a similar condition being imposed on the subsequent purchaser.

Disclaimer

This book is a work of non-fiction. However, some names and identifying details of individuals have been changed to protect their privacy. Any resemblance to actual persons, living or dead, or actual events is purely coincidental.

Table of Contents

Dedications — 1

Acknowledgments — 3

Preface — 5

Chapter 1
    The Beginning of the End — 9

Chapter 2
    Journey of Hope in Warsaw — 25

Chapter 3
    A Triumph of Love — 37

Chapter 4
    Beyond The Sorrow — 57

Chapter 5
    Beyond The Memories — 75

Chapter 6
    Solace in The Shadows — 91

Chapter 7
    In Pursuit of a Miracle — 103

Chapter 8
    The Dual Dance — 121

Chapter 9
    The Fake Color -- 139

Chapter 10
    Navigating Worlds Apart ----------------------------------- 151

Chapter 11
    Between Life and Legacy ----------------------------------- 165

Afterword -- 185

Dedications

This memoir is lovingly dedicated to my sons, whose love and support inspire me every day, and to my childhood friend, Sabir, whose companionship, and resilience have profoundly shaped my journey.

ECHOES OF FATE

Acknowledgments

I extend my deepest gratitude to my family and all those who have steadfastly supported me throughout my life's journey, especially during its most challenging moments. Your unwavering support and encouragement have been the cornerstone of my resilience and growth. I am profoundly grateful for your love, guidance, and presence, which have illuminated even the darkest paths. You are the true heroes of my story, and I am forever thankful for your belief in me.

ECHOES OF FATE

Preface

"In the end, it's not the years in your life that count. It's the life in your years."

-Abraham Lincoln

Over the years, numerous friends and colleagues urged me to write down my life story, some even volunteering to do it for me. Yet, I consistently brushed aside the suggestion, feeling that my life's tale, while unique, might not be extraordinary enough to merit its own book, perhaps filling just a handful of pages. Back in Darfur, where I grew up, everyone's life is marked by remarkable experiences and challenges, making me hesitant to set my story apart. Additionally, I harbored concerns that in the so-called developed world, where daily life often revolves around seemingly less significant issues, readers might struggle to connect with the depth and meaning of my experiences.

Last summer, during a family vacation, I experienced a moment of unexpected inspiration. As we relaxed together, I enjoyed a few glasses of Mamajuana, a traditional Dominican drink known for its potency. In this light-hearted atmosphere, my children seemed particularly fond of my more relaxed demeanor, reveling in the stories and humor that flowed as easily as the drink. Amidst our shared laughter and tales, an idea crystallized in my mind, one that was both clear and profound. It was in that moment, surrounded by the warmth of family and the ease of the evening, that the concept for "Echoes of Fate" was born.

"Echoes of Fate: From Birth to the Last Heartbeats" transcends a mere collection of true stories; it represents a deep dive into the core of my existence. The process of writing this book was deeply personal and empowering, as it involved confronting and transcending my traumas and fears, transforming them into a narrative of strength and courage. It required not only my courage to uncover long hidden wounds but has also provided healing. This process guided me toward profound self-awareness and reconciliation with my past. Like a therapeutic vessel navigating through the stormy seas of life's experiences, this book has been instrumental in fostering a deep understanding and healing of my soul.

In "Echoes of Fate," I weave an introspective journey into the core of human existence, defying traditional perceptions of strength and vulnerability. This memoir goes beyond merely recounting life events. It explores the profound complexities of human resilience and persistence. It challenges the idea that tenacity is innate, and portrays it instead as a facade, as a mask carefully constructed from life's adversities. This mask offers protection from the world's harshness but also veils a rich mosaic of emotions, fears, and vulnerabilities. My journey illustrates how this mask serves as both a survival mechanism and a barrier to our deepest fears and desires. The narrative invites you to moments where this facade cracks, exposing the pure, raw essence of our humanity. Here, strength is reinterpreted not as the absence of vulnerability but as its courageous acceptance and integration into our being.

Guiding you through my early years, shaped by its challenging environment and cultural norms, you will follow my path from the rugged landscapes of Darfur to the global stage. The narrative traverses the complexities of global immigration, stark disparities between nations, and the influential role of fate in shaping our destinies. This journey is more than a battle against a life-threatening condition or the struggles in remote corners of the globe; it's a testament to the human spirit's remarkable capacity to endure, adapt, and find meaning amid life's unpredictability. Weaving together themes of love, loss, legacy, faith, and identity, I invite you to reflect on your own journey and to see the world anew.

Through the narrative of this book, I invite you to embark on a journey that transcends the typical memoir. This one is a rich tapestry of my life, interweaving not just events and people, but also the profound reflections and emotions that have shaped my existence. It begins in the heart of my mission in Iraq and spans continents, confronting the stark reality of human mortality.

While crafting this memoir, I've come to understand its importance goes much deeper than just recording life's events. It's a formidable instrument for personal freedom and a means for societal conversation. It gave me the strength to dismantle my barriers, letting my voice elevate the unspoken and turn soul's whispers into global declarations. Through this process, I have tackled personal challenges and societal concerns, making each word a stride toward liberation and recovery. More than just a way to express myself, writing has evolved into a connector to a wider audience, fostering discussions that surpass cultural and societal limits.

I proudly share my opinions and perspectives in this book with sincerity that may challenge, or even infuriate some readers. As the narrative born from moments of profound introspection, particularly when confronted with the imminence of death, my perceptions of life underwent a dramatic shift. It is through this lens of heightened awareness, stripped of any superficiality, that I narrate my story. This narrative is direct in its approach yet unapologetically heartfelt, it dives into the complexities of life. It aims to foster open dialogue, encourage critical thinking, and perhaps inspire others to explore and share their own life stories. At its core, this book is a forthright exploration of life's profound truths, approached with both respect and sincerity.

"Echoes of Fate" is a legacy that I crafted for my sons. As you turn these pages, I've poured out wisdom and life lessons, captured during times of uncertainty and introspection. This unfiltered narrative of my life is not only a guide for them but also a way for them to understand their father and the world he experienced. It's a candid revelation of my journey, embodying the hopes, dreams, and values I wish to impart to them. This legacy, written at a juncture where every breath was precious, is a heartfelt testament to the enduring bond between a father and his sons, offering them a beacon to navigate their own paths in life.

Welcome to "Echoes of Fate: From Birth to the Last Heartbeats," a narrative that promises to leave a lasting impact on your heart and mind, inspiring reflection long after the final page is turned.

CHAPTER 1

The Beginning of the End

"YOU ARE GOING TO DIE," said the doctor from behind his massive wooden desk. He sat there, breathing heavily, beads of sweat cascading down his bald head and along his face, like a tropical rain. His large body barely fit in his armchair, his expansive stomach pressing against the desk. He resembled a Japanese sumo wrestler.

Behind him, the wall was decorated with several framed certificates, each a testament to his academic and professional achievements. One indicated that he had earned his master's degree in cardiology in the United Kingdom and another that he was a member of the Royal Cardiology Association in that country. Yet, he was the unhealthiest healthcare worker I had ever encountered, a living contradiction to his profession. The irony of his condition was so striking that I almost felt compelled to suggest he seek medical advice, only to catch myself with the amusing realization that he was a doctor himself.

Upon hearing his statement, I couldn't help but respond with a touch of sarcasm, offering a wry smile as I quipped, "We're all going to die one day, aren't we?" His demeanor was grave as he calmly listened to my thoughtless response, which wasn't surprising given that earlier that day, I had candidly confessed to the nurses about my continued heavy smoking and drinking habits.

He leaned further back, pressing into the small armchair beneath him. It seemed as though the chair might cry out in protest. When he opened his mouth to speak again, Arabic words struggled to emerge from his throat. "What kind of work do you do?"

I explained my job as a humanitarian aid worker, emphasizing my specialization in emergency responses in war-torn areas. As I spoke, I endeavored to convey the heavy stress associated with such work, partly in an attempt to justify my smoking and drinking. Despite my efforts, he appeared largely disinterested, his attention seemingly elsewhere as he promptly moved on to another question without much acknowledgment of my explanation.

"Do you have money?" he inquired, a sudden shift in his tone.

His question struck me as odd and out of place. Was he trying to understand my financial capability to afford costly medications or treatments? I patiently explained that one of the benefits of my job is comprehensive international medical insurance. I detailed how it covers all necessary medications and medical procedures, extending even to emergency evacuations if required. I hoped my comprehensive answer addressed his question.

He listened with a lack of evident interest, though he courteously allowed me to complete my explanation. Taking a few sips of water from the bottle on his desk, he paused for a moment, then looked at me and said, "As I said earlier, you're going to die." He inhaled deeply before continuing. "Very soon. At most, you have two or three months left."

The room was enveloped in a heavy, tense silence that lingered for a couple of minutes, amplifying the gravity of the moment. Finally breaking the stillness, he continued, "The results of the tests and exams we conducted this morning indicate that you have severe and chronic heart failure. The imaging also reveals that your heart looks like a rotten tomato, and no medical procedures on the planet can fix it."

After a brief pause, he seemed to recall something else. "By the way, you should know that you have fractured two ribs on your right side, a result of your intense coughing. The best we can do for this is to offer you some painkillers to manage the discomfort."

Once more, the room descended into a profound silence. The usual sounds of the bustling street outside, the muffled voices of other patients in the corridor—all seemed to vanish, leaving me in an isolated bubble of quietness. A wave of emotions cascaded over me, a mix of disbelief and shock. I felt almost weightless, as if my body were floating in an ethereal space. A strange sensation washed over me, an inexplicable feeling of heat and cold coursing through my body. I found myself questioning if I were still breathing. Amidst this whirlpool of sensations, a single drop of sweat began its descent down my back, distracting me as it traveled from the top of my spine all the way down my back.

The doctor broke my concentration on that damn drop of sweat, saying, "When I asked about your job and financial standing, I was only trying to know your financial situation to understand if you could feasibly stop what you are doing and return home to be with your family for the remaining time you have." He paused, then added, "I assume you have a wife and children."

I nodded in agreement.

"So, here is my advice," he went on. "Don't bother pursuing further medical treatments; it would be a waste of both your money and time. Simply go back to your family, wherever they are. If you are short on funds, do whatever you need to do, but ensure you spend these remaining weeks with them."

I remained silent, staring at him in disbelief, my mind racing yet unable to form a coherent response. Then he added, "I'll prescribe some medications to support your heart function. While they may not reverse the condition, there's a possibility they could extend your life by a few weeks. I'm sorry to deliver such news. I wish things were different." He paused for a moment, his expression reflecting empathy. "I truly wish you the best in the time you have."

With those words, he extended the prescription towards me and offered his hand for a handshake, a gesture of professional respect and human compassion in the face of life-altering circumstances.

****

Three days earlier, on the evening of Monday, September 11, 2016, we had just returned from a dinner outing and found ourselves gathered in the living room of a generously sized two-story villa in Erbil, Iraq. There were my two colleagues: Kevin, hailing from Tasmania, and Dan, a Canadian. Joining us shortly a few minutes later was Layal, a Lebanese citizen, who, while not officially part of our team, shared a personal connection with us as Dan's wife.

Although we were coming from difference corners of the globe and diverse cultural backgrounds, we found common ground in our shared experiences within the humanitarian sector. These experiences not only united us but also gave rise to numerous humorous anecdotes. Dan and Kevin were both veterans in landmine clearance with over two decades of experience. The fact that they each still possessed all their fingers and toes was testament to their expertise. The three of us—Kevin, Dan, and I—were sent to Erbil for a critical and challenging mission. Our task was to clear the landmines laid by ISIS along the main access roads in northeast Syria. The goal of our operation was to open a safe humanitarian corridor, connecting northern Iraq-Kurdistan to northeast Syria.

As the night's heat enveloped us, dry and intense, we sat exchanging humorous stories and experiences. Our laughter echoed through the room, escalating into a loud chorus that only seemed to become louder with each tale shared. The discussion naturally shifted towards the more serious aspects of our mission, focusing on the looming threats posed by ISIS in both Iraq and Syria. We talked about the scary reality of being potential targets for live executions on social media, a realistic contrast to our earlier lighthearted banter.

Earlier that day, we had analyzed samples of landmines retrieved from Syria, marveling at their simple yet lethal designs. ISIS deployed these devices randomly as part of their strategy, turning everyday locations into deadly traps. Often, these landmines were stacked, one on top of the other, complicating our task. This random and insidious approach to mine placement required us to exercise extreme caution, which slowed our progress as we meticulously worked to ensure safety while clearing these hazardous areas.

The conflict in northeast Syria during 2016 was a nightmare of violence and complexity, its complexities sometimes beyond even my understanding. The actors in that area had transformed it into an exceptionally complex and harrowing disaster, with serious humanitarian consequences for the innocent civilians trapped amidst the relentless situation.

The primary actors in the conflict included:

(1) The Syrian Democratic Forces (SDF)—a coalition of Kurdish, Arab, and other ethnic militia groups primarily led by the Kurdish People's Protection Units (YPG). The SDF were focused on fighting against ISIS and aimed to establish autonomous regions in northern Syria.

(2) The Islamic State of Iraq and Syria (ISIS)—a radical jihadist militant group that had taken control of large areas of Syria and Iraq. Their primary goal was to establish a caliphate and impose their extreme interpretation of Islamic law.

(3) The Syrian government—led by President Bashar al-Assad, who sought to regain control over all territories in Syria, including areas held by rebel and Kurdish forces. Assad received support from Russia, including military aid and airstrikes.

(4) Turkey—led by President Recep Tayyip Erdogan, who was mainly concerned with countering the Kurdish forces and who viewed the YPG as an extension of the Kurdistan Workers' Party (PKK), a Kurdish separatist group fighting in Turkey.

(5) Various rebel groups fighting against the Syrian government—some groups were aligned with moderate factions seeking democratic reforms, while others had Islamist agendas.

(6) The International Coalition—led by the United States, the coalition supported the SDF and other forces in the fight against ISIS by providing military assistance, airstrikes, and training.

(7) Russia—led by Vladimir Putin, who supported the Syrian government and conducted military operations in Syria, targeting both ISIS and other opposition groups.

****

Before starting the mission, Kevin and I had our first meeting in Manchester, UK, for an orientation and pre-deployment onboarding session. Over the course of three days, we engaged in comprehensive briefings and meticulously laid out our operational plans, prepping us for what lay ahead. We then flew for 7 hours to Erbil, with a brief stopover in Istanbul, a relatively short journey compared to other extensive travels for such missions. For instance, a few weeks earlier Kevin had a marathon journey from Tasmania to Melbourne, then on to Dubai, London, and finally Manchester, all just for a three-day briefing.

However, the flight to Erbil presented its own challenges, particularly for Kevin. Being an XXXL-sized individual, he struggled with the confining space of the economy class seating. Observing his discomfort, the flight attendants kindly provided a seatbelt extension to accommodate his size. Luckily, the middle seat between us remained vacant, offering a bit of extra space. Despite this, I couldn't help but notice a part of him trespassed on my space. It made me wonder how someone of Kevin's size manages the demanding task of landmine clearance, which necessitates adopting various positions—sitting, lying, and squatting—often for extended periods.

Our flight landed in Erbil late in the evening. Dan, who had travelled from Canada and arrived a few days earlier, was there to welcome us at the airport. He drove us to where we would be staying—a spacious villa strategically located opposite the US Embassy. For the time being, this villa was to be solely occupied by Kevin and me, with other team members scheduled to join us in the coming weeks.

For security precautions in the event of any kind of attack on the villa, we decided that Kevin would occupy the westernmost room on the first floor—he also hated stairs due to his weight—while I took the room at the eastern end of the villa on the second floor.

As we settled into the spacious villa, it quickly became a hub of activity and camaraderie. Our living room turned into a space for planning and unwinding, buzzing with the energy of dedicated professionals. Despite the serious nature of our mission in a conflict-torn region, the villa evolved into a sanctuary where we could regroup, recharge, and prepare for the challenging tasks ahead, strengthening our bond as a team.

ASSIM SALIH

****

Around 10 p.m., Dan and Layal decided it was time to end their evening, so they headed over to the embassy across the street, where Layal's organization had provided accommodations for her and Dan. Not long after their departure, Kevin and I cleared away the beer bottles and leftover snacks. We exchanged goodnight wishes and retreated to our respective rooms.

That night coincided with Eid Al-Adha, a profoundly significant holiday in the Muslim world. In Erbil, this auspicious occasion is celebrated with a three-day official holiday, embracing the spirit of joy and reverence. Bearing this festive period in mind, I had indulgently planned to relish a leisurely sleep-in the following day, immersing myself in the tranquility and festive atmosphere of the holiday.

It only took me a few minutes to fall into a deep sleep. However, a sudden fit of coughing woke me up. I felt a blockage in my throat and tried to clear it. I drank some water, managed to calm my throat for a moment, and lay down on the bed. However, within moments, the coughing resumed, becoming more intense. The spasms were so strong that I found it hard to breathe. I tried to go to the bathroom, a few steps away from the bed, but the extreme weakness drained my energy, making walking nearly impossible. "What was going on? I was totally fine all day" I said to myself, pondering.

The intensity of the cough escalated, and a sharp pain radiated from my right side. When I looked at my reflection in the bathroom mirror, I saw a teary face, runny nose, and eyes that seemed to be on fire. I was breathing hard in the middle of a fit of coughing, but I managed to spit into the sink. The scene before me left me horrified.

Almost a decade prior, I underwent open-heart surgery due to complications from an accident I experienced as a child. Five years later, I had a second open-heart surgery to correct a side effect from the initial procedure. These two experiences provided me with a great deal of knowledge about cardiology, my body, and how it works. Although I don't claim to be a cardiologist, I knew more than most people.

Upon examining my own spit in the sink, I immediately realized the problem that was the cause of the violent coughing. My spit turned a distinct shade of pink. "Damn, I had heart failure!"

My extensive experience with cardiology issues and having undergone two open-heart surgeries had made me well-versed in my own heart condition. Thus, at that moment, I realized that my heart could not efficiently draw blood from my lungs and circulate it throughout my body. This explained the weakness I was feeling. My body was starving for oxygen. The cough was the result of blood left in the lungs because not all the blood was being drawn to my heart. Some remained, causing discomfort in the lungs, which, in response, began to fill with fluid to filter the blood. Along with heart failure, there was a looming danger that my lung problem would quickly develop into pneumonia. The severity of my condition stunned me.

Desperate for Kevin's help, I tried to leave my room. But my weak condition prevented me from even reaching the door. Surrendering, I lay on the bed and grabbed my cellphone to call Kevin. From across the villa, I could distinctly hear his snoring. His phone ringing was equally audible. After several calls, it was clear that nothing would wake him up. Due to the nightly curfew set by the local authorities that limited movement from 11 p.m. to 6 a.m., reaching out to Dan, our driver or anyone else seemed pointless.

"Man, calm down and think," I told myself.

Whenever I travel, I carry emergency medications, and luckily my medication pack was right next to the bed. Searching inside, I found two Lasix pills, although they had expired some time ago. But given my critical condition, the expiration date seemed acceptable. Lasix, also known as Furosemide, is a remarkable diuretic used to treat fluid build-up in the lungs resulting from heart failure. To my understanding, Lasix aids the heart by eliminating heavy minerals from the blood and expelling them through urine—minerals such as potassium and sodium, among others. I was immensely relieved to have even that expired medicine within arm's reach.

Over our careers, those of us in the humanitarian emergency professions sometimes undergo training sessions for professional growth and for acquiring new safety and security skills. While some of these sessions prove invaluable, I must admit that most fade from memory almost immediately, dismissed as irrelevant. I once took a self-medical care course during my military service. Though it was informative, that was still 15 years ago, and I had mostly forgotten the content—until that night. From what I recollected, in my current state it was best to lie flat on my back, elevate my feet and upper body using pillows. This position, counteracting gravity's pull, would facilitate smoother blood circulation and ease the heart's pumping function. The combination of Lasix and the laying position really helped; the coughing subsided, and my breathing began to return to normal. Despite a mild sudden fever, I regained enough strength to alternate between resting on the bed and visiting the bathroom.

I lay there until dawn, hoping for stability. However, a concerning thought struck me: the next day was Eid Aladha. In Iraq, many health facilities would typically remain closed, and most doctors would be on holiday. This wasn't Europe; during such significant festivities in Iraq, patient care often took a backseat.

Eid Aladha holds a huge significance in the Muslim world. Often referred to as the "Big Eid," it's the most celebrated occasion in Islam. For me, it's been tinged with gloom since December 30, 2006, the day of President Saddam Hussein's execution. My stance on Saddam was neutral; I was at that time detached from the world of politics and largely oblivious to the events in Iraq—or, for that matter, any other nation. His execution neither delighted nor disturbed me.

What cast a shadow over that particular Eid Aladha in 2006 was the live broadcast of Saddam's execution, which I watched from start to finish at my home in Sudan. Despite witnessing many harrowing events and encountering numerous casualties due to war or disasters in my line of work, this was the first time I had seen an actual hanging execution. It was deeply unsettling.

I can't pinpoint when it began, but for at least the past two decades, before I watched Saddam's execution on television, I've been haunted by a recurring nightmare. In it, I am executed in my mid-thirties. Due to the dream's vividness and the horrifying terror, it always kept me from sharing it with anyone—a burden I've carried in silence. This nightmare would repeatedly resurface, serving as a grim reminder of a foreboding fate. Witnessing Saddam's execution intensified the nightmare's grip on me.

And now, here I was, in my mid-thirties, in Iraq, on the morning of Eid Aladha—struggling to keep my heart beating, struggling with the strange parallels between my current situation and Saddam's final moments, both happening at the same hour. A chilling thought crossed my mind. "Is this just a coincidence? No, definitely not a coincidence. This is my end. This is my fate. This is the nightmare that I kept having for years, and it is becoming real. Probably this is my last breath, and my soul will fly away at any moment."

I began to panic, with fear and terror rapidly consuming me, further aggravating my already horrific condition. My breathing became more rapid and heavy, and the painful coughs intensified. Every part of my chest ached, and I felt paralyzed, pinned to the bed by the weight of my symptoms.

Suddenly, the sound of a toilet flushing broke the silence. Kevin's up! All those beers last night! I gathered my strength to call out his name, but my cries were met with silence. Reaching for my phone, I dialed his number. I could hear his phone ring, but there was no answer. On my second attempt, he finally picked up.

"Man, what is your deal calling at this hour? It's 6 in the morning!" His voice bristled with irritation.

Pushing through my coughing, I managed to say, "Kevin, I'm dying. Heart failure. Please, come now." Words then failed me, replaced only by more violent coughing. He seemed to hesitate, but my persistent cough was the only response.

Given Kevin's hate for stairs due to his weight, we had agreed upon his occupancy of the first-floor room when we first arrived at the villa.

Climbing even a single flight was a lengthy challenge for him. Yet, when faced with my life-threatening situation, he appeared at my door in what felt like seconds, bursting in with urgency.

Despite the gravity of the situation, the sight of Kevin was almost comical. There he stood, stomach hanging over his baggy underwear, eyes wide and bloodshot, hair wild and looking like a fat Einstein. He looked as though he just completed a marathon. Though the scene before me begged for laughter, it was no time for humor.

The seriousness of the situation became clear to Kevin when he saw my condition. Curiously, even though I felt a little relief, I tried to appear resilient in front of him. I didn't want him to see my panic. Between the coughs, I filled him in and explained my trouble and how the Lasix had been my lifesaver. That's when he mentioned he too had a stash of Lasix, "No wonder with that weight he carries he has Lasix as well." I thought.

Our knowledge about how things worked in Erbil was quite limited since we were relatively new to the country. However, we were lucky to find an Iraqi fixer who was our go-to for all local matters. Fifteen minutes after Kevin contacted him, he was in my room. To be honest, I had reservations about Erbil having a hospital equipped to treat my condition. Nevertheless, I asked him to check for any potential hospitals, clinics, or cardiologists for consultation, either over the phone or in person. Given that it was Eid, we were all aware of the slim chances of anyone being available. I also handed him a list of medications to get, emphasizing their importance.

A few hours later, he returned. Predictably, he hadn't been able to connect with any doctors or find reputable healthcare centers.

But he did come through with the medications: Lasix for reducing the heart's load, Warfarin to thin the blood and prevent clots, and antibiotic injections to stave off severe pneumonia. I took a moment to appreciate my own resourcefulness—diagnosing my condition and self-prescribing, though I certainly wouldn't recommend this approach to anyone.

The next three days were manageable thanks to the medications. Occasional coughs, some pain in my chest, and intermittent fever were all I had to deal with. However, my energy levels were low. The same staircase that Kevin hated became my enemy as well. Thankfully, our fixer scheduled an appointment for me with the city's best cardiologist for the morning of our fourth day in Erbil.

Conveniently, the cardiologist's clinic was just around the block from where we stayed. Right on time that morning, I reached the clinic, where the nursing staff promptly conducted preliminary tests: blood work, an echocardiogram, an ECG, a stress test, and an X-ray. Once done, they asked me to return in the afternoon after the test results had been analyzed, and that was when doctor I had never met conveyed the horrible news and told me, "YOU ARE GOING TO DIE."

CHAPTER 2

Journey of Hope in Warsaw

I was skeptical of the doctor in Erbil. For heaven's sake, he lived in Iraq, light years from the advancements of modern medical science. Observing his own unhealthy condition, it seemed he might be closer to death's door than I. Perhaps he was ill informed, and the certificates decorating his office walls were either fabricated or outdated. I was confident that European doctors would challenge his diagnosis, that they would find my condition just a minor issue that could be easily resolved. I envisioned myself back at work in Syria in just a few weeks.

Having grown up in the small town of Darfur, we often viewed medical opinions with a bit of skepticism. It wasn't a disregard for science and medicine but more about the absence of access to well-trained doctors unless one traveled to the larger cities. Interestingly, in Darfur, we held health workers in high respect—even those nurses with only six months of training. They were considered almost like doctors. However, seeking medical assistance at a hospital or clinic was not routine and was typically considered only when someone had been seriously ill for an extended period.

When illness struck a family member, our default was the wisdom of our elders. Interestingly, many educated individuals in Darfur possess a broad knowledge of diseases and medicine, equaling, in some respects, to the expertise of primary care doctors in the US. When I reference "educated" here, I am referring to those who are literate and hold a high school diploma. For instance, a person displaying mild malaria symptoms would be accurately diagnosed and prescribed Quinine tablets or, in severe cases, administered an IV. These nurses employed a minimalistic approach—capturing information from a brief conversation, perhaps touching the patient's forehead to measure their temperature—and voila, a diagnosis and prescription are provided. It makes one wonder why others around the world invest so much time, money, and effort to become doctors! Of course, just kidding.

One morning when I was eight years old, my mom took me with her to visit one of her friends who had been admitted to the hospital. The visit went well; her friend was recovering. A qualified doctor was present in the ward, and several of those nurses trained only for six months were moving around. However, what truly stunned and frightened me that day occurred as we were leaving the hospital. At the gate, I witnessed the hospital guard performing surgery on a little girl about my age, right under the hospital wall's shadow. The young girl was squatting, her face tilted upwards to the sky, her mouth awash with blood. The guard stood over her, using sharp, locally made tools, extracting small pieces of flesh from her mouth. The girl tried to scream, but only a gurgling sound emerged due to her bleeding. She attempted to move, but her mother disciplined her, urging her to remain still. This terrifying scene did not attract any attention by the passers-by. Perhaps everyone assumed the guard was a competent surgeon simply because he worked at the hospital. I recognized him as a hospital guard because his son was a classmate of mine in school.

Sometimes, my people avoided seeking professional medical treatment out of fear or embarrassment. Take one of my neighborhood friends, Ashraf, for example. In his mid-20s, he began showing symptoms of hemorrhoids. However, he hid his condition, fearing the thought of surgery. His situation worsened daily, and eventually he confided in his close friends. We would offer him various traditional treatments every time we heard of one, hoping that he would recover. After a period of absence, I returned to my hometown to find out he had finally sought medical help. The diagnosis confirmed hemorrhoids, and he urgently underwent successful surgery.

My friends later told me what made him take this unusual step. It was because one of the traditional treatments he tried aggravated his condition. Someone had suggested a bizarre treatment: deep-frying a live frog until it became crispy, drying the fried frog, grinding it into powder, mixing it with some of the frying oil used for frying the frog, placing the mixture on a cotton pad, and inserting it rectally overnight. Desperate and in pain, Ashraf took this advice to heart, and, unsurprisingly, woke up in even more pain the next morning, which ultimately led him to the hospital.

When I had the opportunity to travel globally, I realized it wasn't just my home community that sometimes avoided professional medical assistance. In Somalia, there's a small shop that sells cigarettes, candies, and balloons where I frequently bought cigarettes while on assignment there. I couldn't help but notice that people frequently described their symptoms to the shopkeeper, seeking his medical advice. He'd offer his perspective and suggest a medication from his shelf, be it pills, capsules, injections, powders, or syringes. Out of curiosity, I asked if he had any medical training. In Sudan, some doctors work as public transportation drivers because it's more lucrative, and I thought maybe that was his case. However, he clarified that he had no formal medical education. He simply noticed the absence of pharmacies in nearby villages and began offering medicines, which proved profitable. Oddly enough, our humanitarian organization ran clinics in those very villages, with qualified doctors and nurses, offering free consultations and treatment. Yet, many locals seemed to trust him over our services, even to the point of being willing to pay for his treatments.

In Java, Indonesia, a friend once questioned me about a distinct scar on my chest. I explained it was a result of surgery. She said that in her community, any sick family member would simply pay a witchdoctor. This witchdoctor would then supposedly transfer the illness from the person to a chicken. In turn, the chicken would suffer or even die in the patient's stead.

There are countless tales and instances of traditional medicines and beliefs worldwide, but that wasn't my case. I was in denial, finding it hard to trust the doctor in Erbil, primarily because his diagnosis terrified me. I was scared and wasn't ready to face the likelihood of dying.

****

When I returned from the doctor with the distressing news, I contacted our headquarters to inform them about the situation. I urgently requested to be flown from Erbil to Poland, where my wife and son resided at the time and where I could access top-tier medical care within the EU. As international staff, our insurance covered all related expenses and facilitated any medical needs until I recovered, up to a cap of half a million dollars. On the other hand, my wife, being an American and a senior employee of an international organization, I was enrolled under her insurance as well, ensuring I could have access to the best consultation available if I were in the US. Moreover, as a taxpayer and legal resident of Italy I was entitled to free medical assistance in that country.

After a week of negotiating with the insurance company, I was finally on my way to Warsaw to reunite with my family and seek further medical advice.

I landed in Warsaw around 2:30 p.m. and reached home a couple of hours later. It was a Sunday, and my wife was at home. She already knew the reason my mission was cut short and why I was back. I knocked on our apartment door, and within seconds, she opened it with our 18-month-old son standing beside her. When seeing me, his eyes widened in surprise for a moment, then he turned around and walked away in what seemed like a huff. It was as if he was saying, "Bro, where have you been? Why did you leave me with this lady?"

A couple of years before that, late 2014, I was in Italy gearing up to travel to West Africa for the Ebola pandemic emergency response, while my wife was in the US for a brief visit, preparing to move to Dublin, Ireland, to start a master's program she had enrolled in. Concurrently, we were considering having a baby. However, she was concerned that the arrival of our child might disrupt her career plans, especially since she had her sights set on a specific position in the European Union. To reassure her, I promised that if she secured the job, I'd resign from mine and become a full-time stay-at-home dad. She wasn't concerned about being in Dublin alone and pregnant, but while she didn't want to pass up the job opportunity, I was equally enthusiastic about the idea of becoming a stay-at-home dad.

A few years earlier, I had the good fortune to be stationed in Bali, Indonesia, for a year. My role was monitoring the migrant search and rescue operations in the waters between Indonesia and Australia. That year was the highlight of my life because of the amazing people I met from all corners of the world. One such encounter was with an Australian family introduced to me by a mutual friend. They were vacationing in Bali and invited me for lunch at their place, along with some other guests. During the meal, I couldn't help but observe that the children (aged 19, 15, and 11) seemed exceptionally close to their father, even more than to their mother. Curiosity got me, and I asked about this dynamic. I learned that when the couple was younger, the husband worked as a restaurant chef while the wife was a rising government employee. After their first child was born, the husband chose to stay at home, allowing his wife to continue advancing in her career. For 19 years, he looked after their children, and during that time, he discovered his flair for writing. This led him to contribute articles to famous Australian magazines and newspapers. But what struck me most was the profound bond he developed with his children during those years. His story planted the seed in my mind about embracing the role of a stay-at-home dad if ever the opportunity presented itself.

Having been raised in Darfur, I was surrounded by people who the environment had hardened. This was particularly the case in the rural areas like the one I grew up in. Showing emotions or feelings is often seen as a sign of weakness. Boys are expected to toughen up, and men are perceived as tough; in many instances, little girls and women are even more resilient and tougher than men. As children, most of us grew up without any affection—no kisses, hugs, or displays of love. The only emotions we commonly encountered were anger and the punishment that followed when we did something wrong. If one of us came home in tears after a fight, our parents would typically administer a strict punishment, giving us a "real" reason to cry, and then send us back outside to finish the fight.

Once, while at a park in Milan, I found myself engaged in conversation with a fellow Darfurian. We observed a tender scene: a loving mother playing with her young children, periodically pausing to shower them with hugs and kisses. This heartwarming scene led us to a discussion about our own, strict childhoods. I shared with him that throughout my youth, I couldn't recall a single instance of being hugged or kissed by either of my parents. The only times I remember I touched my father was while I was giving him foot massages or when he slapped me in the face for a wrongdoing.

My friend's story, however, was even more striking. He came from a large family—33 siblings, all fathered by the same man but born to four different mothers. He was the eleventh, if my memory serves me right. He recounted that, in all his years in that household, he never witnessed his father display affection towards him or any of his siblings. Whenever a child approached their father, he'd turn them away with a stick and shoo them back to their mothers or call one of the mothers to retrieve her child.

Reflecting on that conversation, my friend's tale of a loveless upbringing, starkly similar to my own, and the inspiring tale of the Australian stay-at-home dad, ignited a profound determination within me. These stories inspired me to rewrite the narrative of my own childhood, to be present and affectionate father with my children, and nurturing a healthy bond with them that transcends time and distance.

Therefore, five months after our baby was born in 2015, my wife secured the job she had been waiting for. At the time, I was in West Africa, engaged in the final stages of the battle against the Ebola pandemic. While I was writing a lengthy email, I was interrupted by the buzz of my cell phone. Seeing her name on the screen was unusual during work hours. I took the call and stepped outside the noisy office. Her voice was full of joy as she shared the exciting news.

"Congratulations, my dear!" I said, "I'm thrilled for you! And remember, I haven't forgotten my promise. I'm going to resign and take care of our son." We concluded the call with an agreement to discuss our plans in detail later.

This was the moment I had been anticipating: the chance to become a stay-at-home dad and to provide for my children what I missed out on in my own childhood. I returned to my desk, saved the draft of the unfinished email, clicked on the new email icon, and within minutes, my resignation was dispatched to my superiors.

The plan was for my wife to hand over our infant son to me in Rome. I needed to spend some time in Italy handling personal matters before I could join her in Poland. From there, she'd head to Warsaw to assume her new role, while our son and I would travel to our apartment in Alghero, Sardinia, marking the beginning of my mission as a full-time father. Given that my son was merely six months old, I naively assumed the role would be a breeze. I envisioned purchasing one of those vibrating baby bed-chairs and spending our days on the balcony—him in his bed-chair, me relaxing in my chair, both of us admiring the view of the Mediterranean. He'd clutch a bottle of milk, and I'd enjoy a cold beer. Evenings would involve walks, movies, and bedtime by nine, allowing me some hours to focus on my writing. If he cried, it would simply signal hunger or a diaper change. It seemed straightforward.

However, a week into our Sardinian adventure, my optimism was replaced with exhaustion. I found myself synchronizing with his erratic sleep pattern—catching some sleep when he did and immediately waking up when he did. I had no idea how helpless and demanding infants could be. They can't sit or walk—they can't do anything for themselves! The similarity between babies and pillows struck me—both are stationary and soft, but while pillows promise rest, babies ensure you're perpetually on your toes.

The most exhausting and exasperating aspect of dealing with babies is their crying, which is particularly frequent during teething. As a parent, it's often impossible to determine the reason behind their tears. The instant my son began crying, I'd be at his side, trying to understand the issue. Check the diaper. Perhaps hunger, even though he's just had a bottle. Could it be a fever? Illness? Gas? Maybe there's something uncomfortable in his bed. Occasionally, in moments of desperation, I'd ask him directly, hoping for a miraculous response. "Can you point to where it hurts or what you want?" Yet the only reply was intensified crying. Almost weekly, I'd rush him to a doctor, fearing something was wrong. And even if one doctor assured me all was well, I'd seek a second opinion from another.

The day he managed to sit upright and hold his head steady, my joy knew no bounds. Now, he could accompany me in the kitchen, playing with vegetables while I did the dishes or prepared his bottle. I got him a seated walker, granting him the liberty to explore our apartment.

For over a decade, I've undertaken challenging roles, lived in harsh environments, confronted gunmen, and handled complex projects. Yet none of that compared to the challenges of childcare. Managing an infant, I realized, resembled running a 50-employee service company where everyone looks up to the top executive. There's HR (baby's well-being), supply chain (baby's essentials), safety (non-negotiable), finance (don't get me started), day-to-day activities (daily outdoor time), routine meetings (lengthy calls with family), stakeholders (doctors, relatives), and the most demanding task: shaping the child's development.

This journey deepened my reverence for mothers, illuminating the sacrifices and patience they embody. I came to understand that mothers, especially single ones, deserve boundless respect and acknowledgment. As for single dads and stay-at-home fathers, my takeaway is simple: just be grateful you don't bear the physical burden of pregnancy and that you're spared the intense experience of childbirth.

Despite all this, my bond with my son began to grow. We weathered good and bad days but managed the time largely on our own. His mother would visit monthly, but he seemed to view her as just another familiar face. He was hesitant to be alone with her without me, perhaps not yet fully comprehending she was his mother. After a few months in Italy, and my personal business resolved, my son and I headed to Warsaw to reunite with my wife.

The challenge arose a year later when I resolved to resume work, taking on a new mission tasked with landmine clearance in northeast Syria. Despite my dedication to stay-at-home fatherhood, the urgent humanitarian call for my specialized skills compelled me to return to work. Therefore, when I was leaving for the mission, I quietly exited our apartment to catch an early flight without waking up my son. Despite knowing he was in loving hands and would enjoy daycare, the parting was heart wrenching. I had grown attached to him over the past year, making the departure even more difficult. However, I hoped that in my absence, he'd develop an even closer bond with his mother.

Three months into my assignment, my heart problems forced my return to Warsaw. It was then that my son's reaction mirrored the sentiment, "Bro, where the heck have you been? Why'd you leave me here?"

ECHOES OF FATE

CHAPTER 3

A Triumph of Love

The day after my return to Poland, I began my medical evaluations. I first scheduled an appointment with a cardiologist in Warsaw. Then, I reached out to a leading cardiology surgeon in Italy who had been monitoring my case for years. My insurance company recommended an eminent cardiologist in the UK, whom I also contacted regarding my situation. Furthermore, through my wife's insurance—which covered me as well—I got in touch with a top-tier cardiology hospital in the United States.

I felt incredibly fortunate to have access to some of the world's finest medical experts. I couldn't help but reflect on how different things might have been had I still been living in my hometown in Darfur. There, I would have been at the mercy of a makeshift medical facility where a guard moonlights as a surgeon. All the doctors—whether in Poland, Italy, the UK, or the US—requested the same medical tests:

blood tests, ECGs, and X-rays. By the end of the day, I had arranged appointments for all the necessary tests.

Within a week, I underwent all the required medical exams, received the results, and forwarded them to the doctors. I felt particularly fortunate to be in Poland at the time. In places like the US, UK, and Italy, it can take weeks, if not months, to secure an appointment for medical evaluations. But in Poland, a renowned private medical company offered exemplary services. In my experience, their level of proficiency and professionalism was amazing. The company has hospitals, clinics, and labs scattered throughout Warsaw. Their call centers were efficient and accommodating. Their infrastructure meets the highest standards, and their services, though top-notch, were relatively affordable compared to other countries. The staff was supportive, knowledgeable, and, crucially for me, English-speaking.

Throughout that week, I noticed improvement in my health. The persistent cough had subsided, my fractured ribs were mending, and my overall health seemed on the upswing. This recovery further confirmed my skepticism towards the doctor in Erbil, leading me to question the accuracy of his diagnosis and to wonder about the potential fatalities that might have resulted from his misjudgments. During this period, I treasured the time spent with my son—walking him to and from daycare, playing at the park, chasing each other, and enjoying meals of chicken nuggets and French fries at the Arkadia Mall. All these moments significantly lifted my spirits.

One day, as I sat on a bench in Krasinski park watching my son chase pigeons, I began to truly appreciate the city of Warsaw. The first time I flew from Milan to Warsaw, I had an entirely different perception of both the city and its people. For some reason, I had imagined it like the Serbian gypsy movie "White Cat Black Cat." Through ignorance, I presumed the lifestyle and cultural advancement of the Polish to be only slightly superior to my hometown of Darfur; the only differentiating factor being white people here and black people there. However, as our plane began its descent over the city, I was struck by the realization of how wrong my assumptions were—a sentiment that deepened once I explored the city. The residents of Warsaw were congenial, the city was modern and advanced, adorned with stunning parks and gardens, an abundance of history and culture, and home to fantastic restaurants and bars. I found myself in love with the city.

A year prior, in October 2015, the right-wing Law and Justice (PiS) party—a conservative, anti-migrant, anti-abortion political alliance—secured victory in the Polish parliamentary elections. Although I was present during this period, I typically kept my distance from the country's political happenings. I do recall that, post-election, US expatriates were cautioned about potential repercussions, especially those of color. Admittedly, I did not care less. The morning after the election results, which had been announced the previous night, I went out for a walk with my son. To my surprise, a few strangers approached me, inquiring about my origins and, despite the political climate, warmly expressed that I, a black man, was indeed welcome in Poland, and showed their gesture with a group hug. Evidently, they were unaware that I was in Poland due to my wife's international diplomatic status and not a migrant. Regardless, their action touched me deeply.

To be honest, it didn't matter whether their sentiments were genuine or whether I was perceived as a migrant. What mattered was the warmth they expressed on that day, which cemented my affection for Poland.

While I felt embraced in that country, globally I was often relegated to the status of an asylum-seeking refugee. (Years previously Italy had granted me official refugee status after a long, drawn-out process.) Regrettably, my welcome wasn't universal, including in my native Sudan. Countries like those in the Gulf even barred me from entry—in part because I carried a travel document under the terms of the Geneva Convention and not a regular passport. Whenever I transited through hubs like Dubai or Doha—a scenario I've encountered over 50 times—I was confined to the airport, irrespective of the duration of my layover. On one occasion, I spent a staggering 52 hours in Dubai airport. Fortunately, I had the means to lodge at the airport's premium hotel.

I have felt unwanted, unwelcome, like a man without a home country for over a decade. The only other time I truly felt embraced was during my first visit to the US months after I married my wife. The warm reception began at JFK airport when an immigration officer, with a broad smile, stamped my passport and said, "Welcome to the United States, brother." That sense of welcome has never ceased.

****

When I received the medical results, I immediately shared them with the doctors. The next day, responses began pouring in. Given the improvements I felt over the week, I was optimistic and expected a lot of positive responses. Interestingly, even though these doctors were in different countries and were unaware that I was consulting all of them simultaneously, they all arrived at the same ominous conclusion:

"There's something wrong, and we need you to repeat all the tests." They provided no further explanations or details.

This wasn't the encouraging news I had hoped for, but I clung to optimism. I reasoned that perhaps the ECG was flawed. Although the other exams seemed routine, errors are always possible. Maybe that could explain why all these doctors wanted the tests repeated? At least, that's what I tried to believe, but a nagging voice inside whispered, "Perhaps the issue lies with you, not the test results." Regardless, I scheduled all the appointments again, this time with different labs and specialists in the hopes of getting different results.

Juggling between dropping off and picking up my son from daycare and shuttling from one lab to another, one clinic to the next, one hospital to another, my fatigue mounted. Because of all the stress, instead of continuing to improve, my health suddenly began to decline. In just one week, I felt as though I had aged half a century. Instead of being in my mid-thirties and fit like a young man, I felt as if I had faded into my mid-eighties or nineties. My entire body ached, and after every 100 feet, I had to pause to catch my breath. I could barely walk, my steps lagging behind me. Stairs became a great challenge, and my physical stature seemed to diminish. On the rare occasions I glanced at my reflection in the bathroom mirror, an astonishing transformation greeted me. Within just five days or so, most of my hair and beard had turned grey. Was this because of my heart condition? Or was it because of the fear and anxiety consuming me?

One morning, after dropping off my son at the daycare, I was slowly walking back to our apartment in the Inflancka area. The sunny yet cool weather, accompanied by the mesmerizing signs of autumn, momentarily made me forget my illness, and I found myself lost in thought. Almost on autopilot, I ended up at Romuald Traugutt park, a scenic expanse not far from where we lived. I tried to cross the park to reach home but was overcome by exhaustion, forcing me to rest on one of the park benches. "Damn, you've grown old, walking like Marianna and Giuseppe," I told myself. Thoughts of Marianna and Giuseppe brought a bittersweet smile to my lips and tears to my eyes.

****

Between missions early in my career in the humanitarian aid sector, I always returned to Italy. This was to see my older son from my ex, who is Italian, to rest for a couple months, and to eat well before embarking on a new mission. My friends, colleagues, and almost everyone I know, love their breaks and vacations. They spoil themselves in relaxation, beach visits, hikes, international travels, or things like yoga retreats in Thailand. However, I'm wired differently. To me, such activities are luxuries reserved for those who can afford them, rather than necessities of life. While many see these luxuries as cures for psychological stress, burnout, or depression, I often wonder about the underprivileged of the world, the refugees in camps, and my fellow Darfurians. I've never heard of any of them falling into depression because they couldn't take a vacation.

Throughout my life, I've never felt any real need for a break. Perhaps there were times I wanted one, but I never felt it was essential. Traveling for leisure, wandering in nature, mountain hikes, attending concerts— while these activities rejuvenate many, returning them to their daily grind with renewed energy, they don't hold the same appeal for me.

In fact, I view an overreliance on them as a sign of vulnerability. Of course, I would enjoy a day at the beach or a hike if I'm with family or friends, but given a choice, I would gravitate towards more purposeful, selfless activities, or simply stay home. I've never felt the need for such diversions to rejuvenate my spirit. Perhaps my resilience, adaptability, discipline, and contentment surpass the norm. I'm constantly fueled by the desire to do good for others rather than seek personal gratification. As a result, I often spend my free time and forced vacations volunteering, eager to stay busy and contribute.

For volunteering, I relied on an outstanding website that was excellent for acquiring new skills, networking, traveling, and finding accommodation worldwide. I engaged with this platform when I felt the urge to travel, socialize, learn new things, and, in return, I would offer my help. However, when I wished to genuinely rest and relax, I usually volunteered at the Valdese elderly care center located in the town of San Germano in the far northwestern part of Italy, close to the Alps. My role there was simple but fulfilling: walk the elderly in the garden, engage in meaningful conversations, and uplift the elderly patients' spirits. I was quite recognizable at the center, mainly because I was the only Black individual there—possibly in the entire town. The elderly residents, unable to remember or pronounce my name correctly, affectionately called me "Giovanotto," Italian for "young man."

The elderly at the center were remarkably kind-hearted. There were no disagreements or arguments, no ego, no jealousy, and no issues whatsoever. This might have been because they recognized they were in the twilight of their lives and believed it best to treat both themselves and each other with kindness. Among them, some had moving stories. Take Angela, for example: a fully capable woman, left at the center by her son and daughter during one of my periods there. They promised to return in a few days but never did. Sadly, she spent her days by the window, endlessly waiting and wondering about their wellbeing.

Then there was Luca, a 96-year-old former member of the Italian Carabinieri (Military Police) suffering from severe dementia. I had to constantly remind him of my identity. Yet, he vividly remembered the details of the Italian invasion of Libya, where, as a young officer, he witnessed the horrendous war crimes committed by the Italians. During this period, hundreds of thousands of Libyans were killed, deported, or interned. But while many residents had captivating tales, the story of Marianna and Giuseppe particularly resonated with me and left a forever mark on my heart.

I wasn't tasked with assisting Marianna and Giuseppe, but I had heard that there was an unmistakable bond between the two. Each morning I'd observe Giuseppe, nicely dressed, making his way to Marianna's room. She'd anticipate his arrival, positioned with her walker at her door. Together, they'd proceed to breakfast and later, the garden. With Marianna leading using her walker and Giuseppe tenderly encircling her left arm with his right, they'd occupy their favorite spot among the roses and melodious birds. They'd spend hours there, chatting and laughing until lunchtime. Post-lunch, Giuseppe would escort Marianna back to her room and retreat to his for a nap, only to re-emerge for an evening stroll and dinner. They always retired to their individual rooms for the night. On special occasions, when the center organized a picnic for those fit to participate, the duo remained inseparable—always seated together, with Giuseppe being the sole assistant to Marianna.

I knew the story of these two lovebirds would be interesting. So, one day after I finished my work, I sat with them and engaged in a conversation. Since then, we had become good friends, and every day I stayed a little longer to enjoy their company. I mostly listened and enjoyed their stories or just sat there watching them argue about a date or something that had happened in the past. It was impolite to ask about their ages, but I learned that Giuseppe was 76 years old, and she was 10 years his senior.

I became more curious about their love story, so I asked them to tell me about it. Marianna said, "Giovanotto, this is a very long story, and it's almost dinner time."

Then Giuseppe added, "Come tomorrow morning after breakfast, and we'll have enough time if you want."

The following morning, even though it was a Saturday, and I wasn't required to be there, I was sitting with them.

When Giuseppe was 15 years old, he was in love with Marianna. She was in her mid-twenties, a beautiful blonde, tall and slender, and stylish. She worked at the Fiat auto factory. As a young man, he did everything he could to impress her and capture her attention. She did notice him but didn't entertain the ideas because of the age difference—he was just a teenager. A year later, she married a wealthy man who took her away from the village, breaking Giuseppe's heart.

Giuseppe thought he had lost Marianna forever, so he moved on with his life. A couple of years later, he joined the Fiat factory workforce. Within a few years, he married and had a daughter who later gave him two grandchildren.

ECHOES OF FATE

After 45 years of marriage, Giuseppe's wife began to experience some psychological and mental issues. Her condition was aggravated when she interacted with people, including Giuseppe. She would not leave the house or speak to anyone except her daughter and grandchildren. It became very difficult for Giuseppe to live in the house, as his wife would become agitated whenever she saw him. Doctors and specialists strongly recommended that she move to a care residence where she could receive appropriate support and supervision. Instead, Giuseppe made a sacrifice and checked himself into the elder center, allowing his wife to continue living in the home where she had spent most of her life. He was almost 70 years old at the time, and he realized that, sooner or later, he would need care anyway.

On his first day at the center, Giuseppe spotted his teenage crush, Marianna, living in the same center. Without any hesitation, he approached her, and immediately their incredible love story blossomed after 55 years of not seeing each other. During those 55 years, Marianna had lived a happy life until her husband passed away, leaving her a substantial fortune in assets, properties, and stocks. She didn't have children or any close relatives, and after a few years, she donated generously to various charities and checked herself into the Valdese elderly center, where one day Giuseppe walked in. Since then, their bond grew stronger, with only death potentially parting them.

As expected, their story was captivating, serving as proof that love always triumphs, no matter how long it takes. A few weeks later, as I left for one of my humanitarian assignments, Marianna had fallen ill, and Giuseppe had moved into her room to be with her constantly. A few days after my departure, I called the center to check on them and was informed that Marianna had passed away on the day I left, and Giuseppe was in poor health. I was told, "He might join her very soon." That was one of the most heart-wrenching moments I'd ever experienced. Overwhelmed by emotion, I locked myself in my room and cried for hours. I never returned to that center.

A couple of months later, I was on the phone with a friend who worked at the Valdese center. She told me that Marianna had written in her will that all her remaining wealth (valued at over 100 million euros) should go to Giuseppe's daughter and his two grandchildren. Marianna also stated in the will that she made this decision because, during her 10 years at the center, Giuseppe's daughter was the only child of any resident who frequently visited her father. Even though she was financially strained, took care of her mother and children, and lived far from the center, she consistently demonstrated her care for her father. Marianna believed she deserved the best for her unwavering kindness to her parents.

****

The day after I sent the results of the second medical tests, I began to hear from the doctors. First, the UK doctor scheduled a virtual conference call. Half an hour before the call, my wife received an email from the US.

The email from the US hospital confirmed that I had chronic heart failure. Based on the results of my two sets of tests, I was in the late stages, and at most, I only had a couple of months to live. My current heart was severely damaged and wouldn't survive another surgery. The only available solution was to get a heart transplant that matched my body's physical and biological requirements. It would be challenging to secure a heart in just two months, but it wasn't impossible. There was a waiting list. However, if a heart became available that met my body requirements and didn't match any of the other people ahead of me on the list, I could be prioritized. To proceed with the transplant, I needed to pay an upfront, non-refundable deposit of $570,000 USD to get on the waiting list. My wife's eyes widened when she saw the amount, but she said, "No worries, the insurance will cover the $500K, and we will work on the rest." She was in shock but tried to comfort me.

I decided to conduct the conference call with the UK doctor without my wife, as I didn't want to risk giving her a heart attack if it was bad news. The call started, and four people were on the other end: two cardiologists, one heart surgeon, and another whom I assumed was from the hospital administration. The news wasn't different from the US email—the same conclusion and the same solution, a heart transplant. There was also the same waiting list issue, and I had to pay an upfront, non-refundable deposit of 385,000 GBP, which was around $550,000 USD based on the daily exchange rate. They then discussed the logistics, including how to fly me safely to the UK, ensuring I lived within a specific radius from the hospital, and having me wear a device around my neck that would notify me as soon as there was a matching heart.

In Italy, I authorized the doctor to discuss the matter directly with my ex, the mother of my older son, to avoid any misunderstandings and to ensure details didn't get lost in translation. English wasn't the doctor's strong suit, nor was Italian mine. A couple of hours later, my ex called. From the first words out of her mouth, I sensed the lump in her throat, hinting at worse news. The difference this time was that the

Italian doctor didn't even bother to mention the heart transplant. He only conveyed his best wishes for my remaining days.

What a terrible day! I felt like I had just received my death sentence, confirmed by the American, British, and Italian medical "courts." It was as if they truly wanted me dead. That was how I felt that day. I wasn't being treated as a patient but as an innocent person sentenced to death, with my only crime being my desire to live.

My appointment with the Polish cardiologist was scheduled for the following afternoon. I had received enough bad news to process for one day, and I assumed his medical opinion and diagnosis wouldn't differ from the others. However, I saw two advantages in Poland. First, I didn't believe they had a waiting list for heart transplants; it was more of a "first pay, first served" system. The second advantage was that I was virtually certain the transplant would cost far less than half a million dollars, which was great news as it would fall within my insurance coverage limits.

I couldn't sleep for hours that night, preoccupied with my condition, the potential solution Poland might offer, and the feasibility of it all. Just contemplating the advantages Poland might provide gave me a surge of hope and made me feel somewhat better, heightening my anticipation to see this Polish doctor. "Everything will be okay. So far, you've weathered every challenging situation in your life. You just need to stay strong and never give up," an inner voice comforted me. Suddenly, I panicked, thinking, "But what if there's no heart available for me until it's too late?" The voice remarked, "Relax and don't worry about that; they will figure it out and get you a heart no matter what. Just refrain from asking too many stupid questions."

ECHOES OF FATE

At some point that night, I reflected on my visit to Erbil. I was reluctant to accept the reality that the doctor in Erbil was right about my condition. I had misjudged him, which wasn't fair. He had detected my condition even quicker than the other physicians. Despite his resemblance to a Sumo wrestler, I acknowledged in that moment that he was proficient and talented in his field. He had advised me, "Don't bother seeking any medical solution for your case. Don't waste your money and time. Just return to your children wherever they are. If you lack funds, sell cigarettes or whatever you can, but spend these last weeks with them." Recalling those words felt like someone had thrown a brick at my face. He was spot-on with the diagnosis, and perhaps his advice was accurate as well.

I glanced at my iPhone screen: it read 2:43 a.m.; craving some fresh air, I dressed and walked outside, dragging my feet. I wandered around aimlessly, consumed with thoughts about the heart transplant. What were the risks? What would the procedure entail? Perhaps it would mirror my previous surgery: I'd drift into sleep, only to awaken days later with an aching chest. What would life post-transplant look like? Would a new heart replace my emotions as well? Would I inherit the donor's feelings? Who would the donor be? Would their gender influence the transplant and my subsequent life?

Lots of questions, with internal voices clamoring for answers and proposing new queries. Suddenly, I realized I was voicing these thoughts aloud. If a passerby chanced upon me—speaking to myself at three in the morning on a dimly lit street in Warsaw, a solitary Black man—it would be an unsettling sight. They might even panic. Imagining their reaction, I burst into loud laughter. Had I just been that audibly reflective? Had I lost my grip on sanity?

After catching my breath from my bout of laughter and coughing, I assessed my surroundings. I was in front of the Polish Security Printing building—the money-printing house. I had to distance myself at once before a guard emerged and misconstrued my presence.

On my return, I remembered the movie "Return to Me," where Grace receives a heart transplant and later falls in love with Bob, the husband of her donor. It was a heartwarming film. I wondered over the possibility of experiencing a similar fate.

I settled into bed, contemplating the doctor's words from Erbil, thinking, "Fuck him. I won't surrender. The Polish option remains, and I'm determined to persevere."

****

Understanding the human psychology is complex. Although the average individual might not understand the complexity of their own psychological mechanisms and its day-to-day impact, many aspects of our daily experiences hinge on our psychological state. This is why some turn to psychologists to gain insights into themselves and seek guidance.

Before diving further into this subject, I must confess that I count myself among those who are largely uninformed about the nuances of psychology and its influence on our lives. In fact, for most of my life, I was a skeptic of this discipline, even going so far as to refer to psychologists as "shrinks." This perspective persisted until my humanitarian mission in Libya introduced me to my colleague, Milia, an incredibly gifted Lebanese psychologist. She never contested my dismissiveness towards her profession or attempted to persuade me otherwise. Instead, she would patiently listen to my ramblings, and at their conclusion offer a brief psychological insight, piece of advice, or opinion—often to my obliviousness. It was a revelation to me when I realized the depth of her insights came from her professional expertise. While I was never formally her patient, she helped me in self-reflection and resolving numerous issues.

We've often heard people remark about a decision, "I'll sleep on it and decide tomorrow," or advise, "Don't rush, just sleep on it." Interestingly, many individuals, after settling on a decision, change their stance the next morning. Why the need to "sleep on it" before finalizing a choice? What role does sleep play in the decision-making process?

I should again clarify that I'm neither a psychologist nor aiming to lecture anyone. My insights are based on readings and articles I've encountered in my efforts to comprehend the phenomenon of people shifting their stance after a night's rest, and I wish to share what I've learned.

This phenomenon seems rooted in three basic psychological and physiological factors—human psychology, hormonal fluctuations, and emotional states. These components vary throughout the day, influencing moods and decision-making. Consequently, a restful night's sleep can provide clarity and sound judgment, prompting some to reconsider their choices.

Additionally, some individuals possess the ability to think unconsciously while they sleep. During this unconscious processing, they might gain new insights or perspectives about their decisions. Stress and anxiety can cloud judgment, leading to impulsive choices.

For some, these feelings diminish by morning, allowing for more rational thinking. We should also consider that we all make numerous decisions throughout the day, which can lead to decision fatigue, causing our judgment to wane by day's end.

These are only a few psychological factors. There are many other elements linking sleep with decision-making. Importantly, not everyone experiences this phenomenon in the same manner. While it might be beneficial to reconsider a decision, frequent changes could also indicate indecisiveness or other underlying issues.

****

After wandering all night, I finally got to sleep around dawn, entirely certain that I'd go for the heart transplant, believing everything would turn out okay. All I needed was to discuss my options with the Polish cardiologist, get the insurance company to cover the costs, and soon I'd have a new heart—hopefully before it was too late.

I awoke around 10 that morning, showered, dressed, and made my way to the Zabka store just around the corner from my building. I purchased a pack of cigarettes, even though I hadn't smoked since that troubled night in Erbil when everything began. From Zabka, I headed to Café Nero, sat outside, sipped a cappuccino, and lit a cigarette. I rationalized: I'll be gone soon anyway—my heart condition, not the cigarettes, would be the mortal cause. Better to find satisfaction and happiness in my final moments than to live with unfulfilled cravings.

My thoughts that morning were dominated by the fat doctor's advice: "Don't bother seeking any medical solution for your case and waste your money and time, just go back to your kids wherever they are." First, did I truly desire another person's heart, a donor about whom I knew nothing? What if the transplant was successful but my life became further complicated for unforeseen reasons? Did I think going through the potential side effects was worth the effort? The entire point of the transplant was to extend my time, to cheat death. Yet, death is inevitable for us all. Why not just accept it gracefully and embrace what comes next? This wasn't the execution-style end that I had imagined over the years, so perhaps it was best to move forward with this natural exit.

By the time I arrived at the doctor's office that afternoon, my thoughts had shifted considerably. Although the will to live persisted, I was quite convinced that I didn't want to carry on with someone else's heart. If there were a heart available that day, I'd prefer it be given to someone else who might benefit more. Given my imminent fate, perhaps this was my chance to donate my other organs, which, aside from my heart, I believed still functioned reasonably well.

Even though I was only in my mid-thirties, I'd lived my life to the fullest. I've traveled the world, pursued education, held a great job, and did my part to alleviate the suffering of others. Yes, I've made many mistakes, but I believe the good I've done outweighs them.

I have two beautiful children. While I'd love to watch them grow up, I'm at peace knowing they'd be in good hands if I were not around; their mothers are exceptional women who I trust implicitly to do right by them. Additionally, I have life insurance worth half a million US dollars. It's not a fortune, but it's a foundation for my children's future.

And let's face it: I've dodged death more times than anyone I know. As a child in Africa, a strange illness claimed my best friend, but I pulled through. In Yemen, an attack took my colleagues, but left me untouched. In Somalia, I narrowly survived a bullet that should have ended my life instantly. In Afghanistan, a last-minute decision to cancel a trip saved me from an attack that claimed all in its path. And in Syria, ISIS never managed to capture me or my colleagues, despite their intentions to use us as a shocking execution for the world to see. It feels as though fate has had an unusual plan for me, always steering me clear of the final curtain. But this time, I'm choosing to face the inevitable head-on, on my own terms.

This is precisely what I conveyed to the doctor, who respected my decision. We discussed the next steps, including medications that would make my remaining time more comfortable, as well as the need for almost daily medical checkups. "Who knows? Maybe a miracle is around the corner," he mused. I left his office with a smile and chose to keep our conversation and my resolution a secret from the world.

CHAPTER 4

Beyond The Sorrow

The feelings and level of comfort one experiences after making a significant decision can vary from person to person. It often links to their confidence in the decision and whether it was the right choice or not.

Choosing not to proceed with a heart transplant was a significant decision. It likely meant facing death sooner rather than later. Nevertheless, I was confident in my choice and accepted my fate. That day, I felt a profound sense of relief and peace. The looming uncertainty about survival was no longer a burden. My thoughts shifted towards what came next: preparation.

Although I had come to terms with my fate, I recognized that those around me might not be as accepting. They might become persistent in their concerns, disturbing my remaining days. So, I chose to keep my decision a secret until the time was right, figuring others already have enough on their minds. This way, they would have no choice but to come to terms with it at a time of my choosing. I wasn't entirely comfortable concealing such a significant part of my life, but it felt necessary. I understood that others might feel hurt or think that I lacked trust in them or hadn't valued their advice. But, in a moment of selfish clarity, I thought, "It's my life, my decision" and found solace in that sentiment.

It was the middle of October 2016, and if I were fortunate, I'd have time only until the end of the year. I began to contemplate my end-of-life arrangements and set my affairs in order.

I reflected on my priorities and found it amusing that at the end of our lives, our list of priorities isn't very extensive. My top concerns were to spend as much time as possible with my children, arrange for my funeral and burial, and decide on the distribution of my sparse possessions. Most crucially, I needed someone who could communicate with my family back in Sudan, someone fluent in Arabic and familiar with our culture, someone I could trust.

Upon arriving in Warsaw, I hadn't anticipated encountering any Sudanese residents. To my surprise, I discovered groups of them living in the city. An older generation had come to Poland to study at the university. After completing their graduate work, many subsequently found work as university professors or in the private sector. Having spent decades in Poland, they had acquired citizenship, married locals, and raised children. These individuals no longer primarily identified as Sudanese, but they kept the culture. The newer generation mainly consisted of students with a few refugees sprinkled in.

Sudanese, by nature, are sociable and maintain personal connections wherever they settle. Yet, after leaving Sudan over a decade ago, I had hardly interacted with my fellow Sudanese back home, mainly due to differences in mindset and political views. I recall my mother often telling me during my childhood, "You do not belong here." In Sudan, I conformed to social norms, joining in whatever those around me did, simply to blend in and not stand out. I had only one true friend, Sabir.

****

The name "Sudan" translates to "land of the Blacks," a description pertaining to the features of its inhabitants. More precisely, "Sudan" refers to the land of people with dark, thick lips. While Sudan boasts a rich tapestry of cultures, languages, and ethnicities, the country has a shared definition of beauty; interestingly, it is often the features that deviate from the typical Sudanese look that are deemed most attractive. The beauty standards in Sudan prioritize soft and long hair, light skin, thin lips, and straight noses. Such traits aren't just beauty benchmarks; they are also linked to social and professional success. This could explain why many Sudanese politicians and celebrities seem to share these looks and often come from specific tribes. Historical perspectives suggest these beauty preferences have deep roots, since certain northern Sudanese tribes were known to have favored White colonizers, initially because their distinct appearance was appreciated.

Sudanese individuals with pronounced dark lips and curly hair often face challenges with societal acceptance. No matter their education or wealth, they might still be seen as being unattractive or less presentable, leading to fewer opportunities compared to those whose features were more acceptable.

By the standards of this society, I was considered unattractive, and this perception shaped much of my experience in Sudan. From neighborhood children to schoolmates, university peers, colleagues, and even neighbors, many likened my appearance to that of Shrek—as in the movie. They would poke fun at my notable nose, small ears, large lips, short curly hair, and deep dark complexion. Compounding these challenges, I had a speech disability as a child and couldn't articulate most words clearly until around the age of four or five. In their eyes, I was the silent, atypical Shrek.

One day, my mom opened up to me, revealing that when I was about three years old, she'd broken down in tears, questioning why God had sent her a child she perceived as unattractive and mute. Was it a punishment for some past misdeed? Or perhaps a test of her resilience? She shared this to emphasize how proud she was of the successful person I'd become, contrary to her earlier fears. I offered her a gentle smile in response, but her words stung and have lingered with me. It's possible that this perception influenced my strained relationship with my father; perhaps he too struggled to accept his "baby Shrek" son.

This sense of being different meant I grew up without genuine friendships. The few friends I did have seemed to remember me only when they needed something. This profound sense of isolation affected my formative years deeply, often making me feel like an outsider within my own community. Yet, on the brighter side, it broadened my perspective, fortified my resilience, and refined my ability to read people's intentions.

My childhood was punctuated by solitude. Even my siblings would mock my appearance during arguments. Deprived of playmates, I sought solace in imaginary friends. The children in my neighborhood rarely invited me to join their social activities and playtime, only doing so when they were short on participants. I often found myself spending hours alone, lost in thought, pondering life, the universe, the mechanics of machines, the nature of electricity, and everything between the earth and the sun. This isolation turned into an academic advantage; with ample time on my hands, I diligently completed homework and practically applied my lessons from physics, chemistry, and math to my daily life. I became the curious "nerd baby Shrek."

****

During the summer break after second grade, I contracted an unusual illness. I had been happily playing with other kids at a wedding, but by day's end, a sharp pain shot through my right foot, with my big toe noticeably swollen. I assured my parents that I hadn't injured myself, but they suspected I had dislocated my toe joint. My father took me to a witch doctor who confirmed their suspicions. She massaged my toe, causing me great pain, and asked my father to bring me back the next evening for another session. The following morning, to my relief, my right foot felt fine. However, the pain and swelling had shifted to my left foot. My frustration grew when my parents refused to believe that it was a different foot. I hoped the witch doctor would recall her treatment from the previous day and clarify the mix-up, but she sided with my parents and subjected me to another painful session. On the third day, both my feet were swollen up to the ankles. Only then did my parents finally believe this was not my fault. A few days later, I was taken to the hospital, where I was referred to Khartoum, the capital of

Sudan, for further medical evaluation. The illness kept me bedridden for weeks, prompting my father to seek treatment for me in the capital.

At the Kuwaiti Hospital in Khartoum, the doctor swiftly identified my condition after analyzing the test results: rheumatic fever, an illness that can inflame the joints, brain, heart, and skin. We had never heard of this fever before in our town, being more familiar with typical tropical diseases and stomach bugs. It seemed fitting that the town's outlier would be the first to contract such a rare condition. I received my medication and returned home. However, due to my limited mobility and a lack of transportation, following the doctor's recommendation, I had to switch schools to one closer to home.

In my hometown, students never brought snacks or lunch to school. With the luxury of an hour-long lunch break, everyone would return home for lunch and then come back to school. This was the norm, even for students with disabilities. However, due to my unique condition, I became the first student to bring lunch to school.

During lunchtime on my first day at my new school, I observed a tall, skinny student in worn-out clothes sitting alone in the shade provided by a classroom wall. It was evident he didn't have lunch or anything to eat. I approached him, introduced myself, sat down, and shared my meal.

His name was Sabir, and he was in the same third grade as me. He had to repeat the grade because he missed the exams for the fourth grade due to an illness. Sabir had recently transferred from another school because of a condition that prevented him from walking long distances. Originally from another region in Darfur, he was an orphan, having lost both parents before turning five. He lived with his uncle, a casual worker supporting a household of 14 mouths, including 11 daughters, his wife, his mother-in-law, and Sabir. Though he lived with them, none of them really attended to Sabir's needs. No one expressed concern over his health or provided him lunch for school.

Despite his challenging upbringing, Sabir always had a smile on his face and a knack for cracking jokes. He was witty, intelligent, mature, and very proud. Although we were in the same grade, he was a few years older than me. He was well versed in all the subjects we studied, often displaying knowledge surpassing that of our teachers.

Sabir was the second person ever to profoundly impact my life. To this day, whenever I face a problem, I often ask myself, "What would Sabir do in this situation?" He taught me many invaluable lessons about life, including controlling my emotions, adapting, and surviving. While I had a challenging and lonely childhood, Sabir's experiences were immeasurably harder than anyone I knew of, yet he never broke down. I never saw him upset or weak; he was always optimistic, positive, and focused on the silver lining. He taught me how to cope with pain, overcome my speech disability, and engage with society without feeling left out. He convinced me that my perceived ugliness and loneliness were my most potent assets, making me stand out in a world where everyone sought to blend in.

We shared lunch every day at school, met up after classes, and spent most weekends together. When I was ill, he'd update me about school, bring assignments to my house, and submit them to the teachers on my behalf. I reciprocated the same care when he was under the weather. Despite knowing Sabir's pride, I tried offering some of my clothes, hoping that I was not bruising his dignity. Still, with immense grace, he always declined. We observed that our symptoms were similar and suspected we shared the same condition. When I proposed sharing my medication, he countered, "If we split the dose, we'll both end up ill. You take the full dose. I'm strong enough to survive."

Sabir was the only true friend I ever had—the brother I always wanted. I vowed that nothing would come between us and that our friendship would last forever. However, as the school year neared its end, Sabir fell seriously ill and missed the exams again. During this time, I visited him daily, sitting with him outside his home for hours, discussing life, and reading books. Even in immense pain, Sabir remained his cheerful, smiling self. As his condition deteriorated and he became bedridden, our chats shifted from outside to inside his traditional house, built from mud and grass and called in the local language a Tukul. Shockingly, none of his family seemed concerned about his health. I pleaded with both his uncle and my father to intervene, but I didn't see any action taken on his behalf.

My visits to Sabir remained consistent, often twice a day, except for one particular Friday. We had guests at our home, and I was occupied assisting my mother until evening. Thus, I resolved to visit him early the next day and spend the whole day with him. Just a little while later, I heard a knock on our front door. I was closest, so I answered it. Standing before me was one of Sabir's older cousins. In a sad tone, she spoke, "I have not seen you today, so I just want to make sure you knew... Sabir passed away this morning."

Shock seized me, rendering me momentarily numb as the reality sunk in. Waves of disbelief crashed against the shores of my mind, struggling to comprehend the enormity of the loss. A deep ache settled in my heart, as if a piece of my very essence had been torn away. Stunned, I turned to my father, who was nearby, my heart pounding with disbelief. "Sabir's dead?" I asked, my voice trembling with shock and anger.

My father met my stare with an emotionless expression. "Yes," he confirmed quietly, "he passed away this morning, and we buried him earlier today."

The news hit me like a heavy weight, and I could feel tears welling up in my eyes. "May God rest his soul," I murmured, before turning angrily away and retreating to my bed. Grief washed over me in waves, engulfing me in a whirlwind of sorrow and anguish. Tears flowed freely, a testament to the profound bond shared with my friend. I felt adrift, grappling with the enormity of my emotions while clinging to cherished memories.

That night, I was engulfed in anger and sorrow. First, I was furious with myself for not visiting him that day, believing that had I been there, he might still be alive. I was upset with my father for knowing about his passing all day yet withholding the news. I was also certain that my mother knew about it too but refrained from telling me, which added to my feelings of being upset with her as well. I resented his family for not caring enough, thinking that their care could have made a difference. I was angry with God, the universe, the angel of death, or whatever force had claimed Sabir's life. I raged at the world's injustices. Why Sabir and not someone else? The boy had suffered immensely since birth. He had lost both parents, lived with a family that neglected him, endured a life plagued with illness, lacked basic necessities, and never truly experienced a carefree day. He deserved a shot at a longer life, a chance to savor some happiness, an opportunity to understand the purpose of his existence. Out of the seven billion people on this planet, why was he chosen that day? Why was he brought into this life only to face misery and then die? Life, what a fucking joke!

I couldn't sleep that night, consumed by anger and rage. By morning, I felt frighteningly calm. I refrained from speaking, even though I sensed my parents observing my every move. After taking a shower, I dressed in nice clothes, had a glass of milk, and rode my bicycle to Sabir's house. I went straight to the spot where we used to sit and read in front of his home. It was there that all my feelings, emotions, and grief converged.

I had just lost the only friend I'd ever had, my brother, my teacher. I lost the only person who truly understood me, stood by me, and taught me how to navigate this harsh world. I was devastated. Tears flowed until they couldn't anymore. In my sorrow, I asked myself, "What would Sabir do in this situation?" The answer became clear. I blew my nose, dried my face, stood up, got on my bicycle, and left.

A couple of months went by; everyone seemed to forget Sabir, but his memories lived on in me. I've never met anyone like him since, nor have I found another true friend.

****

In Warsaw, I sought out the Sudanese community for some sort of social contact and to remind me of better times in Sudan. On one occasion, I met Ali. He had lived in my hometown in Darfur during his childhood, and although we were perhaps too young to recall if our paths had crossed, his father was one of the instructors who trained me at the military academy. Some other Sudanese guys helped babysit my son during my medical checkups. They knew I was ill, but they were unaware that I only had a few weeks to live. However, Ali and I connected on a deep level, making him the closest Sudanese friend I had in Warsaw.

After much thinking, I asked Ali to meet me one afternoon at Nero Café on Inflancka Street. We settled into a quiet corner with our coffees, and I told him the gravity of my medical situation and the decision I'd reached. Ali listened attentively, his face betraying his shock, but he remained supportive and understanding. Once I finished, he asked with a shaky voice, "So, what do you need from me? How can I help?"

I laid out my needs: first, in the event I fell into a coma, became unable to communicate, or passed away, he would serve as the primary contact to relay information to my family back home. My wife doesn't speak Arabic, and they would undoubtedly have many questions. The second matter was the disposition of my remains: burial or cremation. Most people discuss these preferences with their loved ones well in advance. However, I hadn't broached the topic with my family, as I didn't want to arouse their suspicions or reveal my decision.

Despite religious preferences, many people go for cremation due to its cost-effectiveness, environmental friendliness, speed, and the flexibility in handling the ashes. In contrast, burial has numerous associated costs, is a slower process, offers less flexibility, utilizes casket materials that can harm the environment, and occupies land that could be repurposed. To me, the typical pros and cons of cremation versus burial didn't hold much weight. Through cremation, my body would transform into ashes, which loved ones could keep or scatter as they wished. Either way, I'd be gone, any distinction between cremation and burial would be petty. But considering that I have depended on earth's resources my entire life, it felt selfish to withhold my body from the same environment that sustained me. I wanted to continue benefitting humanity and the environment after my death, whether through donating my organs, contributing to medical research, becoming nourishment for worms, acting as a natural fertilizer, or potentially becoming a minuscule fraction of oil over eons. If humans had always chosen cremation, we might never have discovered remains like Lucy, other hominid fossils, or learned anything from ancestral burial sites like the pyramids. Although I'd decided on burial, there were still factors to consider ensuring my choice remained considerate and practical.

When someone passes away abroad, their body is often repatriated to their homeland for burial, in line with their tradition, culture, and religion. However, based on my experience in the humanitarian sector, I understood the complexity of this process. The bureaucracy, paperwork, permissions, fees, and other logistical challenges can be overwhelming. I've always strived to avoid inconveniencing others in life, and I certainly didn't wish to do so in death.

I told Ali that my wish was to be buried in Warsaw or wherever I might pass away. To minimize my environmental impact, I wanted a Muslim burial: no casket, no metals, no clothes, just wrapped in a simple white cloth and placed directly into the earth. It wouldn't matter to me whether I was buried in a Muslim, Jewish, or Christian cemetery, or even a simple grave in an unmarked location; to me, earth is earth. I then lightened the mood with a jest: "At least the soil in Poland is cooler and more refreshing than the hot African soil in

Sudan. Here, I can rest and relax alongside these dead white people." This joke brought a smile to Ali's face and elicited a laugh.

We continued our conversation for a little while longer. When he left to attend to his own affairs, his face bore a look of concern and sorrow. I felt guilty for placing such a responsibility on Ali, but he was the only person I could turn to and trust.

****

Death is inevitable, and everyone will face it sooner or later. However, the uncertainty of its exact timing forms an essential part of the human experience. This uncertainty prompts individuals to be mindful of their choices, maximize the value of their lives, and spend quality time with their loved ones. This unpredictability profoundly influences people's behaviors, emotions, wellbeing, and daily life decisions. Still, whether someone wishes to know the time of their death varies based on their beliefs, perspectives, and coping mechanisms.

The theory of terror management, a concept within social and evolutionary psychology, suggests that all humans harbor a fear of death. This fear significantly shapes our lives. Being aware of the timing of one's death intensifies anxiety about our limited existence, reminding us of our mortality. Such anxiety propels individuals to seek meaning in their lives, find solace in their beliefs, and pursue immortality through their accomplishments and legacies.

People adopt various coping mechanisms when confronted with the knowledge of their imminent death. Some find comfort and relief by seeking emotional support from others or engaging in spiritual and religious activities. Others might invest time in self-reflection, appreciating the life they've led, and making the most of their remaining days. However, what truly terrifies people about death isn't necessarily the knowledge or uncertainty of its timing. The most profound fear lies in the unknown that follows death and the question of what comes next.

Based on religious and ancient history, only a few have reportedly returned from the dead, with Jesus Christ being the most renowned example. The New Testament of the Bible recounts the resurrection of Lazarus by Jesus, a tale central to Christian belief. The Hebrew Bible (or Old Testament), also referenced in the Quran, narrates another resurrection tale: a widow's son who was brought back to life by the prophet Moses to identify his murderer. However, upon doing so, he immediately returned to his death. There are other stories of resurrection in Buddhist texts, as well as in ancient Egyptian and Greek mythologies. Yet, no resurrection has been recorded in modern history, and contemporary science has been unsuccessful in reviving the deceased.

Strikingly, not a single person who supposedly returned from the dead has provided a detailed account of what follows death—neither Jesus Christ, Lazarus, nor the widow's son. Our knowledge of the afterlife is primarily sourced from holy scriptures, personal beliefs, and various theories. To date, no scientific evidence or firsthand testimony confirms these accounts. This uncertainty about the afterlife is what instills fear in many when contemplating death.

✶✶✶✶✶✶✶✶✶✶

After my meeting with Ali, I felt relieved and satisfied with my arrangements. Only one significant priority remained: spending time with my older son who lived with his mother in Italy. It was just a one and a half hour flight from Warsaw, then a two-hour train ride from Milan. Not too bad, I thought. I picked up the phone to inquire if my medical condition would allow me to fly. The Polish cardiologist's response was clear: "Absolutely not. Your heart is performing at around 25% compared to a healthy heart. It might quit during airplane takeoff." His response shocked me and was a stark reminder of my limited time left.

I reached out to my son's mother, asking if she could bring him to Warsaw. Without hesitation, she agreed. Knowing my son holds Italian citizenship brought immense relief. If he had been in Africa with a Sudanese passport, he probably would not been able to visit, leaving me without a final goodbye.

Citizens of the USA, EU, and other countries like Singapore, Canada, Norway, Australia, and the UAE might not realize the power and privileges their passports bestow. They can easily book tickets online and travel to their chosen destinations. Not only are they granted easy access to most countries, but they're also treated with respect and dignity upon arrival. I have heard of two Sudanese individuals working in Saudi Arabia at the same organizational level. However, one earns a salary five times higher than the other only because he holds a British passport. In fact, many American nationals in the UAE lead comfortable lives, with their primary qualifications being their US passport and native English proficiency.

These passports are so powerful and valuable that they can make their holders prime targets for kidnappings for ransom. I have never heard of someone from Bangladesh, Zambia, Sudan, or Somalia being kidnapped for ransom—perhaps the only advantage their nationality could offer. These nationals are worth nothing to the kidnappers, and their respective governments might not prioritize their retrieval. While I was in Malaysia, I encountered a man who bought stolen passports. Curious, I asked him how much he would pay for a Sudanese passport. He responded, "I wouldn't take it even if it was free. It's useless."

The optimal time to obtain a passport in Sudan is right before high school graduation, since students need a government ID to sit for their final exams. Years ago, I was chatting over the phone with a high school peer. As I recounted my global travels, he fell silent for a moment. When he finally spoke, he asked, "Do you remember when we got our passports?" I confirmed that I did. He then confided, "Since that time, I have applied for visas to every country in Europe plus Canada, Australia, China, and several other countries. Every application was rejected." After a touching pause, he added, "From the moment I received my passport, I haven't been able to leave Sudan, not even by a single meter." It was evident from his voice that he was on the verge of tears as he continued. "I don't even want to settle abroad. I just want to see what people in these countries look like. After that, I'd happily return to Sudan."

That's the unfortunate reality of the visa and immigration system in our world. Some nationalities enjoy the privilege of traveling wherever and whenever they want for any reason, while others aren't entitled to those same privileges. These strict immigration rules and visa requirements restrict people from certain countries or regions, leading to inequality in opportunities for mobility. Citizens of wealthier or politically powerful nations enjoy more freedom of movement than those from economically disadvantaged or politically unstable countries.

One of my humanitarian missions involved search and rescue operations in the Mediterranean Sea, and it was among the most heartbreaking experiences I have ever had. I witnessed people drowning or fighting for their lives in the middle of the waves. Parents watched their children die before their eyes, helpless to save them, surrounded by countless floating bodies. Regardless of why these migrants risked their lives, whenever we brought the survivors to European shores, the Italian, French, and Greek governments often denied our ships docking privileges, and even when we were granted permission, these survivors were often treated inhumanely, while we, the rescuers, were viewed as criminals.

These rules and requirements have placed the lives of many legitimate asylum seekers at great risk because they were unable to flee their countries. Numerous people have died because they couldn't seek better medical assistance elsewhere. This has resulted in family separations, provided opportunities for criminals and human traffickers, and forced many to risk their lives in migration attempts.

I am not advocating for the elimination of visas, borders, or immigration rules, nor am I suggesting that people should move freely between countries without any order or regulations. However, the way these systems have been designed and regulated primarily serves and benefits certain nations. For example, developed countries often attract only skilled and highly educated individuals, facilitating their immigration. This leads to what is called brain drain, impacting the labor force, economic growth, and workforce diversity in the migrants' countries of origin. This, in turn, can result in poverty and humanitarian crises, pushing people to seek migration—an option that's often not available. What a disgrace!

While this might sound selfish, I am profoundly grateful that my two children don't have to experience such injustice and inequality since one is an Italian citizen and the other an American.

CHAPTER 5

Beyond The Memories

Now that both my sons are with me, and I've settled all my affairs, my focus is only on each moment of my remaining days. My daily routine involves spending as much time as I can with family and friends, adhering to my medication schedule, and attending doctor's appointments. Most importantly, I need to let go of my worries and embrace the present joyfully.

As of today, the first week of November 2016, my elder son, is 9 years and a couple of months old, while my youngest, is just 18 months. My elder son and I share some memories, but the youngest is too young to have formed any lasting recollections of our time together. Regrettably, neither child is familiar with my life story, the challenges I've faced, or the man I've become. There are countless life lessons, values, insights, and untold stories that I wish to share with them.

Unfortunately, I have no close friend or family member who truly understands me. I've kept a significant portion of my life and personality hidden, never allowing anyone full access to my deepest thoughts or the vault of my secrets. Neither my parents, siblings, the mothers of my children, ex-girlfriends, friends, authorities, supervisors, colleagues, doctors, nor anyone else possesses the complete narrative of my life. Indeed, I am the sole bearer of many vital truths about my character and experiences. While I haven't deceived anyone about who I am, I've also never revealed everything. There's always been a part of me that is a mystery, providing me with a sense of freedom and vitality. Without that, I'd feel as exposed as if I were walking naked in public.

I once believed that my reserved nature and behavior might signify some form of psychological disorder or mental irregularity. However, after extensive research and study, I realized that it's completely normal for some individuals to keep certain life facts and experiences private. This tendency can be shaped by various factors, including individual personality traits, cultural norms, past experiences, and personal boundaries. It is a perfectly healthy behavior as long as it doesn't harm one's overall wellbeing or prevent the formation of meaningful relationships with others. Interestingly, there isn't a specific scientific name or definition for this kind of personality.

There are, however, certain psychological elements and personality traits that could lead one to be as discreet as I am. Factors such as introversion, a preference for privacy, past traumas or negative experiences, trust issues, cultural and social norms, fear of judgment or rejection, a desire for self-protection, and specific coping mechanisms come to mind. I believe I have most, if not all, of these traits, which have played a role in shaping who I am today.

I feel compelled to address this issue before my time is up. I want my children to know the authentic me, not just the version shared by others. While we have numerous photographs capturing our joyful moments, they remain silent memories. Would recording a video or capturing my voice be the answer? Such formats could prove challenging to edit, consuming a vast portion of my remaining time. Entrusting someone with this responsibility would be risky, too. They might misinterpret my words or perhaps even forget the nuances of my tales.

I have been thinking about this all day, considering every option, and at last, inspiration struck: "Why not write a book for them to discover in their own time?" And so, here I am, documenting some of my journey, hoping to complete it while time is still on my side.

****

Let's start with my parents. My mother, a dignified woman, hailed from a humble background. She dedicated herself to teaching primary school children and was adored by her students. While of Nigerian descent, she spent her entire life in Sudan. My father, on the other hand, came from a rich family. A highly educated man, he pursued advanced studies in the UK. Like many from privileged backgrounds, he could be a bit arrogant, sometimes acting as though he stood above others. In truth, my parents' narratives aren't particularly divergent from many families in Darfur. Yet, the truly remarkable tales come from my paternal grandfather and maternal grandmother.

My grandfather was among the first educated generation in Sudan. He worked for WHO—the World Health Organization—and, notably, played an important role in establishing WHO's presence in Africa. Recognized as a genuine humanitarian, he was deeply respected, admired, and cherished by those he worked with and the communities he served. During one of my humanitarian missions, I went to Vonjama, a remote town in the northeast of Liberia, where I encountered an elderly health worker. After a series of questions about my name, lineage, and origins, prompted by my uncanny resemblance to someone he knew, we deduced that he had worked alongside my grandfather. Overjoyed by this revelation, he insisted I accompany him home after work for some barbecue and share some palm wine. Once there, he sent his son to fetch a former colleague who had also known my grandfather. The two spoke for hours, regaling me with tales of my grandfather's hunting passion, his great skill in tracking, stories that showcased his innate kindness, and anecdotes highlighting his counsel to them—advocating for their self-worth and encouraging them to challenge, rather than blindly follow, directives from their European counterparts. They fondly recalled his unwavering ethics, values, and his sheer commitment to his profession and peers.

The two men were in the beginning stages of their careers when they first encountered my grandfather. They were stationed in isolated areas within the dense African bush, and my grandfather made it a point to visit them monthly. These visits not only allowed him to monitor work progress and assess needs but also to distribute wages. With the absence of banking or postal services in these remote regions, many staff members chose to entrust a portion of their earnings to my grandfather, asking him to deliver it to their families. "He never turned us down," one of them recalled. "He'd often use his own money to cover the travel expenses and would undertake these journeys during his personal time. And even with all that effort, he strongly refused any compensation for his troubles."

The other guy chimed in. "Despite the deep trust we had in him, he always insisted on protocol. We'd sign a document detailing the amount he was taking for our families, and by the next visit, he'd present us with a receipt bearing our families' signatures."

I once attended a workshop in Nairobi, Kenya, on humanitarian principles during emergency responses. One of the facilitators, an elderly American who had spent decades in the humanitarian sector, struck up occasional conversations with me during our breaks. I could sense he recognized my grandfather in me, though we didn't discuss the connection in depth. On the final day of the workshop, as he was delving into ways to mitigate risks of corruption, particularly challenging in societies already steeped in corruption, he remarked, "I wish everyone could be like this young man's grandfather." To my surprise, he was pointing straight at me. He continued, "He was an extraordinarily faithful and honest individual." It's truly commendable to be remembered and leave a lasting impression based solely on one's ethics and values.

Although I didn't have a deep personal relationship with my grandfather, my mother always spoke of him with immense respect and admiration. When I was six years old, just a year before I started school, he proposed to my parents that I accompany him on his travels. Though I was young, certain memories and the lessons he imparted remain vivid in my mind. For months, it was just the three of us: a driver, my grandfather, and me, journeying through the African wilderness in a Land Rover, traversing rivers, mountains, and deserts. I knew he was affiliated with WHO, but as a child, I couldn't understand its significance. Yet, wherever we went, local communities would light up at his presence. They recognized him and greeted him warmly.

Apart from the thrilling adventures, he instilled in me values, ethics, and a perspective on life's purpose. One day, after a series of questions about the essence of life, he told me, "If you are under the impression that our sole purpose on this earth is to seek happiness and enjoy in life's pleasures, you are mistaken. We are here to accumulate knowledge and skills that empower us to assist one another and contribute to humanity's progress towards a brighter future." He underscored the importance of education, noting, "Your family isn't wealthy, nor does it hold any social significance. Hence, education is your only ticket to rise above and beyond your circumstances." He then added, "Anything you possess or earn in life can be taken away, but the knowledge in your head is inviolable."

I recall one instance when we were dining at a restaurant. A couple of men walked in, dressed fashionably, and wearing gold watches and shoes with gleaming embellishments. Leaning closer, my grandfather murmured, "Eat what brings you joy, and wear what makes you look sharp." On a different occasion, he reiterated this sentiment but with a twist, saying, "Eat what fills you well, but don't wear what makes you look unwell." He continued, emphasizing the value of personal growth, "Don't spend your time polishing your shoes; instead, focus on sharpening your mind."

When discussing our extended family, he remarked, "Our folks often have a negative attitude and frequently resort to saying "NO." Always strive to maintain a positive outlook and seek the silver lining." He paused for a moment before adding, "If ever questioned about your competence in executing a specific task, refrain from giving a definitive "YES" or "NO." Instead, promise to give it your all, and then ensure you do."

One day, as we sat in an office, I overheard staff members fervently debating their favorite politicians. Turning to me, he advised, "Never merely adopt the opinions of others. Forge your own beliefs and stand by them, influencing others to respect and perhaps even adopt your viewpoints. They're no wiser than you." On another occasion, he posed a question, "Do you know why these people hold me in such high regard?" Without waiting for my reply, he explained, "Because I believe in treating all with respect, regardless of their occupation, societal status, political affiliation, or wealth. I ensure that I extend dignity and courtesy to everyone without exception."

One invaluable lesson from my grandfather remains etched in my memory, a lesson that profoundly shaped my life. One afternoon, he took me out for lunch and ordered a beverage I had never seen before. It was amber-hued, cold, fizzy, and served in an unfamiliar bottle. He demonstrated the proper way to drink it: "Don't gulp it down; instead, let the rim of the bottle rest on your lower lip and sip gently." I followed suit, but the fizz rushed up my nose, creating a burning sensation, causing my eyes to water. Observing my reaction, he asked if I enjoyed it.

"I love it, though it's a bit burning. What is it?" I queried.

He replied, "That's Pepsi." This was my inaugural encounter with Pepsi and other sodas, drinks that were unheard of in my hometown.

A few days later, as I impatiently waited for my grandfather to finish a meeting, temptation led me to snatch a few coins from the top of his desk. Eagerly, I dashed to the same restaurant, a mere block away from his office. My intention was to order a Pepsi, but I had forgotten its name. I described it to the waiter as the "amber-colored, cold, fizzy drink in a distinct bottle." The waiter, suppressing his laugh, handed me a Pepsi bottle. After enjoying the drink, I returned to the office to find my grandfather in a heated discussion with his colleagues over the missing coins. Fear consumed me, prompting me to tearfully admit my transgression. He consoled me, then gently conveyed the importance of not taking others' belongings without seeking permission.

In my remorse, I confessed it was an error in judgment, to which he responded, "The true mistake isn't in making the mistake itself, but in persistently continuing it."

Throughout my numerous humanitarian missions, too many to count, I've collaborated with a variety of people from varied cultures, backgrounds, and professions. While it's not my intention to boast, I can assert with confidence that I stand out as one of the most proficient managers and leaders in the humanitarian emergency response field. Every mission I've undertaken has exceeded expectations for success. Whether it's my teams, beneficiaries, government authorities, or anyone else I've encountered, I've consistently earned their respect and admiration. This excellent track record, my leadership skills, the unwavering ethics I brought to my role, and my unwavering dedication all trace back to my grandfather and the invaluable lessons he imparted during that formative period I spent with him. His influence molded me, creating the person I am today. Truly, he was a remarkable individual.

****

Hawa, born and raised in the sub-Saharan desert of northeast Nigeria, hailed from a tribe of nomadic Muslims. Based on tradition, she married at a young age. With her husband, they soon celebrated the birth of their first child, a tender baby girl. However, their joy was fleeting. A severe fever claimed her husband's life, leaving Hawa a young widow, clutching their infant daughter to her chest. After a period of mourning, Hawa, filled with determination and faith, decided to undertake a pilgrimage to Mecca on behalf of her late husband. Along this journey, loaded with both physical and spiritual challenges, she made her way to the sacred city accompanied by a group from her tribe.

In the 1950s, transportation infrastructure in Africa was not developed enough to facilitate long-distance journeys. Many pilgrims from West Africa, intent on visiting Mecca, traveled on foot across the entire continent until they reached Port Sudan on the Red Sea. From there, they would board ferries to continue their journey. Such a trip could last up to 12 months, with approximately six months spent on each leg of the journey. The hazards were numerous: countless individuals lost their way and were never seen again, while others, captivated by the communities they encountered en route, decided to settle in various villages or towns. Tragically, many surrendered to exhaustion or illness along the way, never completing their intended pilgrimage.

After several challenging months, Hawa found herself in Darfur, Sudan. Traveling with a baby added layers of difficulty to an already hard and long journey. Soon, she fell gravely ill, and her group sought shelter at a remote eatery established especially for the weary pilgrims and travelers who travel that route.

ECHOES OF FATE

The members of the group, aware of the tight schedule to reach Mecca within their intended time frame, delayed their journey for a couple of days in the hopes that Hawa would recover. However, as days passed, her condition did not improve. The elders faced a challenging decision. Leaving her and her child behind seemed the only option, but according to their traditions, it would be disgraceful to abandon her in the company of an unrelated man.

The owner of the establishment, a young man known for his kindness and generosity, had been attentive and helpful throughout their stay. Recognizing the dilemma, the elders approached him with a proposal. If he was willing, they suggested, he could marry Hawa, ensuring she would be under the protection and care of a husband. Moved by compassion and seeing the depth of Hawa's strength and spirit, the young man agreed.

A simple ceremony was conducted on the golden dunes of the desert, binding Hawa and the restaurant owner in matrimony. As the group resumed their journey towards Mecca, they left behind a frail Hawa, her baby girl, and her new protector—a newly minted family in the middle of the vast expanses of Darfur.

After the group left, Hawa slowly regained her strength, the mist of her illness dissipating. But as clarity returned, so too did the shocking realization that she was now married to a man she didn't know—moreover, one whose language she didn't understand. Confusion, fear, and anger gripped her.

In her distress, she repeatedly tried to flee the village, driven by a deep-seated desire to reclaim her freedom and escape her imposed fate. Every few days, In the dim light of dawn or the mysterious veil of dusk, she would run away in a random direction, determined to put as much distance as possible between herself and the unfamiliar life that had been chosen for her.

However, each time the villagers, well intentioned though they might have been, would mount their horses and chase after her. They would find her, sometimes exhausted, sometimes defiant, and bring her back to the village. This cat-and-mouse game continued for weeks, with neither side willing to yield.

Yet, as time went on, Hawa began to notice the consistent kindness and patience of her new husband. Even amidst her outbursts and escape attempts, he never raised his voice or treated her with anything less than respect. It occurred to her that this man, though a stranger, was genuinely concerned for her wellbeing. He made efforts to communicate, using gestures and the few words they had in common, showing an unwavering patience that slowly began to bridge the challenge of language and culture between them.

Hawa's anger and fear began to recede, replaced with a grudging respect and a cautious hope. While she mourned the loss of the narrative of her previous life, she began to see a possibility for happiness in this unexpected new chapter. Over time, the bond between the two grew, built on mutual respect and shared experiences. And while her life in Darfur was very different from her nomadic beginnings, Hawa found solace and strength in her newfound family.

A year into her new life, Hawa welcomed another baby girl into the world. However, fate had one more twist in store: her second husband passed away shortly after the birth of their daughter. Once again, she was now a widow with a baby and a young child. Walking back to her tribe seemed impossible.

Given her circumstances, she made the decision to stay put in the village. She took over the responsibilities of the restaurant her husband had left for her and assisted her countrymen in their travels. She served them hearty meals and tended to the sick. Because she had heard many stories from other pilgrims who had traveled back and forth from West Africa to Mecca, she was often able to provide invaluable guidance to her customers on the safest routes to take. Her restaurant became a beacon of hope and rest for weary travelers, and she found solace in the connections she established with her fellow Nigerians and other travelers.

As years went by, her restaurant grew in reputation. Travelers would speak of the kind widow in Darfur who became a guardian angel for others on their journey. Through adversity, she had found purpose and strength, carving out a legacy in the sands of the desert that would be remembered for generations.

One fateful day, a group of men from Northern Sudan walked into Hawa's restaurant, their eyes searching the premises. Upon seeing her, they inquired about her late husband. When she informed them of his death, she saw a mix of shock and sadness in their eyes. Identifying themselves as her husband's cousins, they told a tale that was as surprising as it was heart breaking.

Her late husband, it turned out, came from a wealthy family in northern Sudan. He was the only son, destined to inherit the family's fortune. However, conflict arose when his father tried to force him into a marriage he did not want. In defiance and desperation, he had fled his home, leaving behind his birthright and identity, eventually settling in the remote village in Darfur where he and Hawa's paths would fatefully cross.

The cousins, far from any enmity, were genuine in their relief at finding the family. They were taken by the beauty and spirit of Hawa's daughters and, seeing the bond between them, invited Hawa and her children to return with them to northern Sudan.

In the luxurious surroundings of her late husband's family home, Hawa was treated with respect and affection. Yet, despite the comfort and luxury, she felt out of place. The stylish rooms and lavish feasts seemed worlds away from the rural charm of her restaurant and the pilgrims she served.

After much thinking, Hawa decided that her heart belonged to the modest village in Darfur. She thanked her husband's family for their warmth and kindness but expressed her desire to return to her restaurant. Respecting her wishes, they ensured she had all she needed to continue her life in Darfur.

Back in her beloved village, life resumed its rhythm. A few years later, destiny introduced her to a man from her own tribe, a pilgrim on his way to Mecca. Their shared history and mutual respect soon blossomed into love. They married and together they ran the restaurant, which had become almost a tradition for many travelers.

Fulfilling her lifelong dream, Hawa, along with her new husband, made the pilgrimage to Mecca. The journey was both a spiritual awakening and a testament to her resilience. On their way back, as they crossed the Red Sea, she gave birth to another daughter. They named her Zamzam, in reference to the holy well in Mecca, symbolizing the blessings and miracles of life's journey.

In the middle of the ups and downs of life, watching countless faces pass through her restaurant, Hawa had learned a significant lesson: the paramount importance of education, especially for her daughters. Aware that knowledge was the key to a better future, she made a difficult decision when her daughters reached school age. She shut down the restaurant that had been her refuge and livelihood, moving to the capital of Darfur, El Fashir, with her daughters and her husband.

The shift was not easy. By day, she worked as a cleaner in a primary school, scrubbing floors and cleaning windows. In the afternoons, she took on the role of a servant for a rich family. Life was tough; she had her husband, who had become sick, to care for, and her daughters' futures weighed heavily on her shoulders. But she bore it all patiently, her spirit never weakened, her resolve never wavering.

All she ever emphasized to her daughters was the importance of their studies. "Focus on your education," she'd often say, "I'll handle everything else. You just study." And study they did. Each of Hawa's daughters pursued her education with fervor, flourishing in their respective fields.

As fate would have it, one of the sons from the rich family Hawa served took a liking to her youngest daughter, Zamzam. Though fascinated with each other, their relationship was met with skepticism from his family due to the difference in their social standings. But love, as they say, conquers all. With the support of his father, the young man married Zamzam, bridging two worlds with their union.

Hawa's journey was one of unimaginable difficulties, solid resilience, and an unwavering belief in a better future. She was a beacon of strength, a symbol of persistence. And as I am writing down this tale, I am filled with pride and admiration. That remarkable woman, Hawa, is my grandmother. Zamzam, the youngest of her daughters, the one who had married the rich son— against all odds is my mother. The supportive father who aided my parents' union is my grandfather, the ethical WHO staff. My lineage is one of love, determination, and endurance.

CHAPTER 6

Solace in The Shadows

While I've made a conscious choice to enjoy each moment and not worry about the uncertainties of tomorrow, there remains a persistent part of me that I can't quite silence. In the daylight hours, I keep these feelings under control by engaging with my family, playing with my sons, visiting friends, and navigating the city for my medical appointments. But as the sun goes down, the darkness envelops the world and, while others find solace in sleep, my anxieties escalate and seem to hold me captive.

During the nights, I am gripped by intense fear and anxieties, haunted by the thought that closing my eyes might mean never reopening them. In these moments of heightened distress, a coping mechanism resurfaces—the voices. They begin speaking to me in my mind, their tones clear and resonant. I find myself engaged in conversations with these voices. Their presence brings some kind of comfort, making me feel less alone in my battle against anxiety.

ECHOES OF FATE

Everyone faces their unique pressures, stresses, and anxieties, each with varying levels of tolerance and coping mechanisms. Personally, I have always had a high level of tolerance and effective coping methods. However, facing my impending death has proven to be more challenging than any situation I've ever encountered, leading to the emergence of these uncontrollable voices.

This phenomenon can be psychologically understood as a form of auditory hallucination, typically emerging in my life during times of heightened stress or anxiety. It's a mental process where my mind, striving to alleviate emotional distress, creates internal dialogues. These voices offer me a mental escape, providing companionship and a semblance of control in situations where I otherwise would feel powerless.

The voices and I have engaged in deep conversations in the past, reflecting on my beliefs and views about the world and humanity. I've experienced moments of passionate and heated debate contrasted by some jokes and laughter. Because I often respond to these voices aloud, I would sometimes need to quietly dress and take a walk, ensuring I didn't disturb my sleeping family.

I'm secretly relieved that these voices choose to visit me only under the darkness of night, sparing others any added concern for my wellbeing. While the world might not understand, these nightly dialogues provide me with some strength and help me cope with worrying situations. I treasure these nightly encounters, and, in their company, I find relief and companionship.

****

Last night, I engaged in a troubling discussion with the voices about religion and faith. This topic had likely surfaced due to my anxiety about death and what might follow, given my situation. The unknown that lies beyond life's end apparently prompted these profound reflections.

Having been raised in a predominantly Muslim society that grew increasingly conservative under El Bashir's dictatorship, the subject has always been a sensitive one for me. In that society, blind obedience was the norm, and everyone was expected to follow without raising doubts. The ethos was one of unflinching obedience, with no room for doubt or questions. That society believed fervently in heaven and hell, with the firm conviction that anyone outside Islam was destined for the latter.

The voices had initiated the dialogue with a series of thought-provoking questions. "How many religions exist in the world? Which are genuine, and which are not? Suppose someone, by fate, is born in a remote corner of the world, untouched by the major known religions—would they be condemned to hell by default?" The voices had further inquired, "Why were Jews and Christians often perceived negatively by Muslims? Aren't they too, according to Islamic teachings, People of the Book?"

When I was in the fourth grade, our study of Islam's fundamentals was led by Mr. Trengasa, the school principal, a devout Muslim with a long history of Islamic teaching in Saudi Arabia, an ultra-religious and extremely conservative nation. He introduced us to the fundamental tenets that define the core of Islamic faith and guide the spiritual journey of a believer. He explained that the Islam Pillars of Faith are belief in Allah, belief in the angels, belief in the holy books including the Torah and the Gospels, belief in the Messengers such as Jesus and Moses, belief in the Day of Resurrection, and belief in Destiny.

At that moment, I raised my hand and inquired, "By believing in the Torah and the Gospel, and in Jesus and Moses, doesn't that make us Jewish and Christians too?" He approached, softly asking me to stand and repeat the question. As soon as I did, a sudden sharp pain struck the left side of my face. He had slapped me—hard! This abrupt action stifled my curiosity, and, with a stern command to sit down and never again ask such "blasphemous" questions, he silenced my inquisitiveness about religion. From that point on, I kept my questions about faith to myself till they were raised by the voices.

In June 2011, during a brief stay in Rome before my next humanitarian mission, I found myself wandering aimlessly on a sunny morning. This stroll led me to the Church of Santa Maria della Vittoria, located near the Repubblica metro stop. Deciding to explore, I entered the church and met Father Tomas, an American priest residing in Rome. He approached me as I was looking around the church, offering a chance for confession. I politely declined, explaining that I wasn't Catholic. When asked about my religion, I simply replied, "I am confused." This sparked a lengthy conversation between us, extending over coffee and lunch, as we chatted for hours.

Father Tomas was not interested in converting me to any specific belief; he was genuinely eager to answer my questions and equally curious to learn about Islam from someone like me, a self-proclaimed confused practitioner. His open-mindedness made our conversation incredibly enriching. We discussed both the positive and negative aspects of our faiths, delving into a deep and respectful exchange about our respective religions. It was enlightening to explore the complexities of faith with someone so knowledgeable yet so open to understanding the perspectives of others.

Parting ways with Father Tomas, I spent the rest of that day immersed in thought. His open-minded approach left me wondering how different the world might be if other religious teachers and leaders shared his perspective. Such an attitude could provide peace of mind to many who struggle with their faith. I found myself wishing my fourth-grade religion teacher, Mr. Trengasa, with his rigid views, could have embraced a similar openness and given me some clarity.

****

One of the voices had seemed to hesitate before asking, "What if the Christians or Jews are right, and Muslims are mistaken?" I had begun answering this question, but caution had spurred me into action. I had quickly dressed and left the apartment to walk the streets, fearing that I might disturb the family. I knew that this would be a lengthy and intense discussion, given its serious nature. At least on the dark streets, I could quietly talk aloud.

After an extended debate, the voices and I had concluded—despite the endless subdivisions within each religion such as Sunni, Shi'a, Catholic, Protestant, and so forth—that if Islam were true, Muslims would be safeguarded, but Christians, Jews, and others would be at a disadvantage due to their lack of belief in Islam. On the other hand, if the Christians and Jews were correct, Muslims should still be in good standing because of their inherent faith in both religions. If only Judaism was true, Muslims would be unaffected, but Christians would be in a precarious position. Similarly, if Christianity held the ultimate truth, then only the Jews would face the consequences, while Muslims would remain unscathed. Theoretically and from a probabilistic perspective, Muslims would always be in a favorable position because, contrary to some perceptions, they are required to believe in and respect other Abrahamic religions, including Judaism and Christianity.

However, the voices and I had immediately dismissed this argument, recognizing that it oversimplified the complexities and theological nuances of religious belief. We had been trying to apply a probabilistic perspective to matters of faith, inherently challenging the essence of belief systems rooted in principles beyond empirical evidence. Our logic had failed to consider the rich diversity and depth inherent in religious experiences and convictions. It's likely that we had reached this point because I was seeking comfort and trying to convince myself that my faith was on the right path.

The conversation had taken a twist when one of the voices posed the question, "What if all religions are merely human constructs, and none are true?" A heavy silence had ensued, as we were consumed by the thought that perhaps we were all damned. Then, out of nowhere, I had burst into uncontrollable laughter, picturing countless souls throughout history killing each other over beliefs in something potentially non-existent. What a bunch of idiots! The sheer irony had been overwhelming. Then I had asked, "Is it possible for an individual to claim they are the 'chosen one' and convince millions of followers based on their narrative? How can such a fabricated story endure for centuries with people still believing in it?"

History is unfortunately full of charismatic fakes who somehow manage to amass legions of unquestioning followers, and Islam is no exception. For example, a Sudanese political leader named Muhammad Ahmad claimed himself to be the Mahdi—"the guided one" in Arabic, a figure in Islamic eschatology who would restore justice and peace before the Day of Judgment. Ahmad led a late nineteenth century revolution against Anglo-Egyptian rule in Sudan. He claimed he was the fulfillment of the prophecy and that he had been sent by God to guide the people. Despite his claims and the large following he amassed, over 140 years have passed with no signs of the prophesied day, leading to the conclusion that he was just an imposter. Yet, millions today continue to believe in him and remain his faithful followers.

The story of the revolution had become a poignant metaphor for my life's questioning of religious belief. Muhammad Ahmad's ability to influence the masses, despite later being exposed as an imposter, exemplifies how charismatic leadership can deeply influence beliefs, especially during times of social strife and scientific naivety. This historical event mirrors the potential of ancient religious figures who in a less enlightened era could have similarly influenced people using charisma and strategic narratives rather than divine truth.

Stories like that had forced me to critically evaluate the foundations of my beliefs. Were they genuinely rooted in divine inspiration, or were they influenced by charismatic figures skilled in exploiting human psychology? Could these beliefs have persisted primarily because they serve to control and manipulate for political and power motives, rather than being the absolute truth?

****

ECHOES OF FATE

Growing up in a society where Islam is not just a faith but an integral part of our identity, children are expected to adhere to its tenets for life. From the moment of birth, they are indelibly marked as Muslims. The unspoken rule is clear: we must remain within the fold of Islam until our last breath. However, for me, the challenge wasn't the religion itself but the prohibition against questioning it. As an intellectually curious individual, I craved evidence or compelling narratives to solidify my beliefs.

I vividly remember a lesson from my first grade, held beneath a tree because we did not have a classroom at the time. Our teacher, Ms. Nadia, narrated the story of Adam and Eve with passion. She described why and how they were expelled from Heaven to Earth for submitting to Satan's temptation and eating forbidden fruit, which she specifically identified as an apple, even though the Quran only calls it a fruit. That narrative, while possibly captivating for my classmates, seemed simplistic and inadequate to my questioning mind, even at that young age. Why an apple? Why did the Almighty choose to forbid something as trivial as a piece of fruit? Could it not have been something more significant, like intruding into a particular area of heaven or engaging in a forbidden practice? Who would banish or punish anyone just because of a bite of a fruit? That didn't make any sense to me.

I began to speculate that perhaps the story of the apple was a metaphor or a simplification of a much more complex event. Over the years it led me to think that perhaps the tale was a cover-up for something more profound, maybe even something as scandalous as an orgy party in heaven. These doubts and questions were not born out of disrespect but from a deep desire to understand and connect with my faith on a more rational and meaningful level. My journey through religion was not just about accepting narratives at face value but also about seeking the deeper truths that lay beneath them.

In our community, tales and parables from other religions were also a common part of our cultural fabric. Not only were stories from Islam shared, but narratives from other faiths were also recounted with a sense of reverence and wonder. We heard about Jesus, performing the miraculous feats of walking on water and turning water into wine. There was also the tale of Moses, who turned his staff into a serpent and parted the Red Sea to lead his people safely to the Promised Land. We were also regaled with stories such as the tales of King Solomon communicating with animals and Jinn.

I have always prided myself on being a man of science, a thinker who values logic and empirical evidence. This scientific perspective naturally led me to critically analyze these religious narratives, which, though rich in moral and spiritual symbolism, often defy the laws of physics and nature as we understand them. In my view science is grounded in understanding the natural laws of our universe, while religion often addresses human behavior, morality, and the meaning of life.

My concerns and skepticism came from an unwillingness to bend the natural laws to validate religious beliefs and persuade people towards a particular faith. While ancient peoples might be excused for their lack of knowledge, it troubled me that many today still accept these miraculous events without critical examination. This unquestioning acceptance among modern, educated individuals challenges my understanding of the intersection between faith and reason.

Now, as I found myself in the twilight of my life, I was confronted with profound introspection. The question that lingered in my mind, casting a shadow of doubt and contemplation, was about my belief. Was I a believer? And if so, what exactly did I believe in? This internal debate was not just philosophical but deeply personal, adding an additional layer of stress to the already heavy burden I bore in those final days.

As the voices and I had continued our unending search for answers, we had found ourselves engaging in questions that challenged the core of religious doctrines. We had pondered the nature of the Trinity, questioning how God could simultaneously embody unity and trinity. The concept of reincarnation had also raised our curiosity—was the soul's journey a continuum, reborn in new forms? We had grappled with the conundrum of predestination versus free will; could everything be predetermined while still allowing for personal responsibility? Then arose the ultimate question: if there were no divine presence, what could explain the complexity of the universe—let alone its origins?

In the profound silence of last night, my mind had been enveloped in intense introspection, magnified by the looming reality of my mortality. This introspective journey had been a relentless exploration of faith and skepticism at its zenith. The tranquility of the night had been transformed into a haven for my deepest thoughts, in which the internal voices—reflections of my own mind—had engaged me in that meaningful conversation. They had become intimate companions in the dialogue that delved deeply into my personal beliefs and doubts.

Here I was in the twilight of my existence, and these reflections had taken on a new urgency. The voices in the darkness, echoing both challenge and comfort, had guided me through a labyrinth of doubts and beliefs. Staying up all night wasn't just for seeking answers but instead had become a journey towards finding peace amidst the uncertainties of faith and reason. However, the exchange with the voices had opened a unique window, allowing me to peer into the depths of my soul, providing clarity and understanding and a rare opportunity for self-discovery and acceptance at a critical juncture of my existence. The dialogue had become a testament to the human quest for meaning, a search that had gained profound significance at the junction of life and death.

As the sunrise marked the end of last night's dialogue with the voices, it left behind a trail of lingering thoughts in the silence, serving as a poignant reminder of our quest to understand our place in the vast tapestry of existence.

CHAPTER 7

In Pursuit of a Miracle

Today, on this Wednesday morning of November 16, 2016, I find myself waking up at an unusual 10:50 a.m. These days, sleep has become a luxury; I often find myself engaged in conversations with the voices in my head deep into the night, only to finally drift off to sleep an hour or two before dawn. As I rise, fatigue clouds my senses. I am overwhelmed by a lack of energy, which makes even the simplest task of getting out of bed seem difficult. There's a troubling decline in my health condition; each time I catch my reflection in the mirror, I feel decades older, almost as if I've aged into my 90s.

"What's on the agenda today?" I wonder, staring blankly at the ceiling. I feel relief because I remember my younger son is at daycare, and the older one is spending time with his mother at the hotel. Good, as I'm hardly in the mood to entertain or have the energy to keep up with them. I love them, but today I am too sick for that. Yet, I remembered my doctor's appointment for an echocardiogram at 3:30 p.m. The constant medical visits seem almost pointless, especially since I know that my last day is just around the corner. Perhaps a shower will help clear my thoughts and help me decide whether to go to the appointment or just cancel.

After the shower, I take my medicines and pour myself some coffee before switching on the TV. As I flip through the channels, I notice that everything is in Polish, except for CNN, BBC, and CNBC. The headlines and breaking news are dominated by stories about Donald Trump being elected the 45th President of the United States, post-election analyses, reactions, and the transition of power. They also cover Brexit, the Syrian war with ISIS, and the European migrant crisis. Finding it boring, I turn off the TV and sit on the balcony, watching people go in and out of the Biedronka minimarket in the building opposite ours.

It's cold and overcast today. November in Warsaw is a transitional month from autumn to winter, with temperatures ranging around 32 degrees Fahrenheit. I'm putting on some warm clothes before calling a taxi to take me to the doctor's office. I don't mind winter and cold weather, but I dislike heavy clothes.

Every time I visit this particular doctor for an echocardiogram, we connect a bit more, and today is no exception. As I step into the room, he greets me warmly, asking about my wellbeing. He's already familiar with my medical history, thanks to our previous appointments.

As the procedure wraps up, he leans in, curiosity evident in his eyes. "What are the other doctors saying about your condition?" I take a deep breath, explaining that their conclusion is far from encouraging—

either undergo a heart transplant or face my death.

He nods thoughtfully before saying, "Heart transplants can be complex. Perhaps it grants you another year before bringing additional complications." After a few seconds of silence, he continues, "Look, there might be another option for you. The best heart surgeon I've ever known is Dr. Andrzej, a German-Polish man. He's mostly retired now, but I heard that he operates a small private clinic here in Warsaw. You should consider meeting him."

His words instantly ignite a spark of hope. "Do you believe he might offer a solution?" I probe.

"If there's a glimmer of hope for your situation, he'll be honest about it," he assures me. Eagerly, I ask for Dr. Andrzej's contact or the location of his clinic. With an apologetic tone, the doctor admits, "I don't have his current contact or the clinic's address. But here is his full name, and perhaps you can locate him online. I'll also do some digging on my end."

I thank him a lot for this lead. With renewed energy, I head home. Upon arriving, I waste no time in opening my laptop to start my search for Dr. Andrzej.

With each click, my hope is increasing. All the results in the search engine led me to The Cardio Clinic, located somewhere on the outskirts of Warsaw. An address and phone number promptly appear on my screen, and, without hesitation, I dial the number. The phone starts ringing, and my chest tightens with anxiety, uncertainty growing inside me.

"Hello?" A female voice breaks through, momentarily catching me off guard.

Gathering my thoughts quickly, I ask, "Do you speak English?"

"Yes, I do," she responds promptly.

What a relief. "I'm trying to reach The Cardio Clinic. Is Dr. Andrzej associated with this clinic?"

"Yes, this is The Cardio Clinic, and Dr. Andrzej is the owner," she replies.

Barely able to contain my excitement, I inquire about the earliest available appointment. The pause on her end feels like an eternity, but when she finally speaks, a mix of disappointment and anticipation grips me. She informs me that they're closing soon and Dr. Andrzej is occupied the following day. However, she suggests a slot on Friday at 1:30 p.m. Without a second thought, I accept.

Once the call ends, a wave of elation washes over me. Strange—I haven't even spoken to the doctor, let alone heard his perspective. Yet real hope grows within me. Could it be that fate is granting me a second chance? Just thinking about it makes me very happy, a contrast to the darkness that consumed me only hours earlier when I awoke this morning.

****

From my perspective, human beings possess a profound ability to regulate their feelings, emotions, and desires. Indeed, what distinguishes humans from animals is our capacity to harness and control ourselves through reasoned thinking. A truly resilient individual can skillfully manage these emotions, basing decisions and daily life choices on practical considerations and risk assessments rather than solely on impulses or feelings. I'm not suggesting that people who are deeply emotional and passionate are weak. However, they can become even stronger if they master the art of controlling these emotions and desires.

Some people might argue my position and believe that emotions are integral to our humanity, serving as the foundation for art, culture, relationships, and personal experiences. They posit that constantly suppressing feelings can harm mental and physical health and rob us of the rich spectrum of human experiences.

However, from my prospective, control does not mean suppression. Instead, it's about understanding and effectively channeling emotions. In many situations, especially professional ones, emotional control is crucial for objective decision-making. This control can also protect us and others from potential harm. Furthermore, mastery over emotions can be seen as a sign of personal growth and maturity.

The ancient Asian philosophies and practices offer techniques to master feelings, emotions, and desires. Meditation in Hindu and Buddhist traditions cultivates focus and clarity. Buddhism's Four Noble Truths and Eightfold Path address human suffering and provide a guideline to manage desires. Taoism, from China, emphasizes harmony with the universe, introducing the concept of "Wu Wei"—action in accordance with nature. Yoga, beyond physical postures, balances the body and mind with its ethical guidelines promoting self-control. Confucianism stresses social harmony through virtue, guiding emotional control. Zen Buddhism, blending Buddhism and Taoism, emphasizes direct understanding and insight. Finally, traditional martial arts, beyond combat techniques, integrate philosophies that emphasize discipline and emotional balance. All these methods promote self-awareness, emotional control, and inner peace through consistent practice.

In essence, while emotions are central to human experiences, the ability to manage them appropriately is equally vital. The key lies in striking a balance between genuine emotional expression and judicious emotional management.

I might not practice meditation, mindfulness exercises, or a physical discipline such as yoga or martial arts. I might not understand anything about the intrinsic connection between the mind and body and how one can influence the other. However, I possess a strong ability to control my emotions, feelings, and desires. I can hone resilience in the face of difficulties, managing myself even when others are overwhelmed.

Growing up in Darfur, we didn't have ancient Chinese scrolls or Kung-fu masters teaching us about emotions, feelings, and desires. Instead, we had a tried-and-true method: good old-fashioned whipping. It's like our own unique version of "mindfulness"!

Ever since I learned about Dr. Andrzej and secured this appointment, my world fills with emotions, feelings, and an inexplicable surge of hope. Every part of me seems to whisper, "He might be your savior." Until this morning, my days were often overshadowed by the thought of inevitable death. But now, rays of hope are breaking through, illuminating a potential future path.

It's funny how emotions work. In Darfur, where we have a more direct (and sometimes painful!) way of controlling our feelings, I'd probably have been in line for a playful whipping right about now. Yet, this newfound hope isn't just about adding more days to my life; it's about enriching the life within those days.

Lost in my thoughts, I daydream about future adventures, family milestones I might witness, and even silly things like finally learning to ski. These strange thoughts somehow make me laugh.

With each hour, my emotions roller coaster between deep reflection and moments of childish joy. My desire to live a longer, fuller life becomes a force I feel within me. Each time I find myself being pulled into the abyss of despair, I am drawn to the idea of Dr. Andrzej and the potential new lease on life he might offer.

The days leading up to the appointment feel longer than all the years I've lived. With every sunrise and sunset, my emotions play tug-of-war between fear and hope. But deep down, I know, allowing my feelings and desires to lead for once might not be so bad. After all, isn't hope the thing that truly keeps us alive?

****

I enter The Cardio Clinic 15 minutes before my appointment. It took about 55 minutes by taxi to arrive here. The reception area is decent, with only a desk and a woman who seems to be the receptionist seated behind it. Although there is space enough to accommodate around 10 people, the room is nearly empty. In the corner of the waiting area, a skinny, short, elderly man sits, munching on what appears to be a chicken salad. Given his presence here and the way he appears, I predict his health condition might be in a similar state to mine. I approach the receptionist.

"Hello, I have an appointment at 1:30."

She replies with a smile, "Yes, please take a seat, and you'll be called soon."

About 10 minutes pass, and the old man finishes his lunch, discards the remains in the trash, and speaks with the receptionist. I can't hear their conversation, but I don't understand Polish anyway. Then he proceeds through a door I presume leads to the restroom. Shortly after, the receptionist calls me to proceed to the doctor's office, and, to my astonishment, she indicates the same door the old man entered.

I knock on the door, and when a voice from inside says, "Please enter," I push it open. The room is modest in size, dominated by a small desk with two chairs positioned in front of it. Sitting behind the desk is the old man from the waiting area, but now he's wearing a white coat.

With a warm smile, he greets me and gestures for me to take a seat. "Do you speak Polish, or shall we speak in English?" he inquires. It's apparent from my skin color that I might not be fluent in Polish, yet he's considerate enough not to make assumptions.

I reply, "English."

As we begin our conversation in English, I detail my medical history up to this point, each diagnosis, and the conclusions offered by previous doctors. He nods in agreement with the echocardiogram doctor, confirming, "A heart transplant isn't the best option." Although the age lines that crisscross his face suggest he's perhaps in his late 60s or early 70s, his demeanor is vibrant, filled with energy like someone much younger. Throughout our conversation, he interjects playful jokes and amusing facts. Yet, he also listens intently, absorbing every detail I share.

At the conclusion of my account, I hand him my thick medical file. He glances at it for no longer than a minute before casually tossing it back to me. "Listen," he starts, his tone shifting to a more serious one, "I don't trust these doctors, nor any results in that file." I sit there, taken aback and silent, words escaping me.

He quickly scribbles down a name and phone number on a sticky note, handing it to me. "This is the only person whose echocardiogram results I trust. Schedule an appointment with him, then come back to see me. We'll take it from there."

Without another word, he stands, signaling the end of our session. I collect my jacket; my face etched with a mix of shock and puzzlement, and I exit his office.

Throughout the hour-long taxi ride home, my mind repeatedly circles back to Dr. Andrzej. Each interaction, every word he said, plays back like a captivating film. His audacious dismissal of my comprehensive medical file, the swiftness with which he directed me to another specialist, and his confidence left an indelible mark on me.

Yet in spite of his quirks and idiosyncrasies, there was a certain magnetism about Dr. Andrzej. His eyes held stories of countless patients, of lives altered, and of his challenges to the conventions of medicine. He had an aura that suggested experience, wisdom, and a hint of rebellion. It was clear that this man had seen it all and yet chose to see every patient, every case, with fresh eyes.

I couldn't help but smile to myself, thinking about his weird nature against his evident expertise. The humor and light-heartedness with which he approached a serious conversation were both refreshing and comforting. He didn't just see a patient; he saw a person. A person with fears, hopes, and a story. And in his unique way, he had given me hope, something that was in short supply these days.

I find myself chuckling, recalling his animated expressions and playful jokes. Despite the gravity of my condition and the uncertainty that lay ahead, there's warmth in my heart. Perhaps it's the newfound hope, or maybe it's just the genuine fondness I've quickly developed for this quirky yet strange doctor.

As the taxi pulls up to my building, I feel a renewed energy. The next steps are unclear, but with Dr. Andrzej in my corner, I feel a renewed sense of optimism. No matter what the future holds, I'm grateful for this unexpected hope in the form of a spirited old doctor.

The moment I step into my home, I reach for my phone and dial the number Dr. Andrzej provided. The voice on the other end crisply informs me that Dr. Andrzej has already briefed him and that I can see him at 8 p.m. at a local hospital not far from my residence this evening. I'm taken aback by the suddenness but appreciate the efficiency. He adds, almost as an afterthought, to bring 600 Polish Zloty—in cash.

Come 8 p.m. I find myself punctually at the location, navigating a dimly lit hospital corridor. I enter a cozy office, dominated by a patient bed and the presence of the echocardiogram machine in one corner.

Throughout my life, I've done countless echocardiogram examinations in various countries in Asia to Europe and Africa, always with the cold touch of the echo handle on my chest. The routine is so familiar that I could probably time the usual 15-minute duration with closed eyes. But tonight, with this doctor, everything feels different, and the session was longer than I anticipated.

He moves the handle inch by inch, inspecting my chest from every conceivable angle. Front, side, back—each area is being scanned multiple times. His focus is unwavering, his concentration is clear. The room is silent, save for the rhythmic hum of the machine and our breathing. Time stretches, and a tingling numbness starts creeping over me from staying in the same position for so long.

An hour and a half later, the prolonged session concludes with him drafting a report, after which he slips it into an envelope, sealing it with a sense of finality. Handing it to me, he insists it's for Dr. Andrzej's eyes only.

Curiosity grows in me, and I can't help but ask about his findings. But he firmly deflects my questions, assuring me that Dr. Andrzej would be the best person to elaborate. Taking the cash, he slides it into his pocket with an air of routine, concluding our session with a simple wish for luck.

As I leave, I'm enveloped in a sense of gratitude. If Dr. Andrzej's recommendation is anything to go by, this was perhaps the most thorough echocardiogram I've ever had. No wonder Dr. Andrzej places such implicit trust in him.

ECHOES OF FATE

****

I am consumed by anxiety about the outcome of the echocardiogram and what Dr. Andrzej will say about my case. It's the weekend, and I must be patient and wait until Monday to find out. To distract myself and spend quality time with my family, I decide to take my little son to the playground at the park.

As he runs around gleefully, absorbed in his own world of fun and freedom, I sit on one of the benches, finding solace in simply watching people go about their lives. At that moment, I feel like a spectator in the theater of life, looking for comfort in the normality around me.

Suddenly, a little girl approaches me, her eyes wide and filled with wonder. I am the only black person in the park at this time, and her expression suggests that she may have never seen a black person before. I wave to say hello, and she waves back, her face lighting up with a curious smile. I playfully stick my tongue out, and she mimics the gesture before giggling and running back to an older woman, whom I assume is her mother or grandmother.

****

This simple, innocent interaction transports me back in time, and I find myself remembering the first time I ever encountered a white person. It's a vivid memory, still fresh despite the years—a moment when the world felt as big and as wonderful as it appears in the eyes of this little girl.

I am not sure how old I was at the time, but it was probably before I accompanied my grandfather on his business trips. I remember it was a little after midday when my mother sent me to the market to buy some supplies for lunch. On my way, I noticed a group of children, their faces lit up with amusement and excitement. They were following a white couple who looked like they were from another world to us—carrying backpacks, wearing shorts and t-shirts, boots, sunglasses, and hats. Everything they wore or carried seemed new and fascinating to us.

I couldn't resist the curiosity inside me, so I joined the group of children, and together, we followed this couple for the rest of the day, wondering who they were and what had brought them here. We were happy, like we had discovered aliens. Some of the bolder children among us tried to cautiously get closer to touch the couple's clothes or skin, but when the couple turned to look, the kids would get scared and run away. The couple themselves seemed just as curious about us. They tried to approach and engage with us, but we would run each time, not quite ready to bridge that gap.

Eventually, the couple sat down under a mango tree to rest, and all of us children did the same, sitting a few meters away, our eyes fixed on them. We sat in a sort of respectful, fascinated silence, simply observing them. A few adults from the village also arrived, gathering behind us, and they were wondering too, looking at these two visitors as if they were characters from a story brought to life.

The lady pulled out something from her backpack, wrapped in golden paper. We watched as she ripped the cover paper away and revealed a flat, dark brown rectangular object. She broke it into little pieces, and our eyes widened in wonder. What in the world was that? She put a piece in her mouth, closed her eyes in a clear sign of joy and deliciousness, then extended her hand and offered the pieces to us.

We were very hesitant to get closer; we just sat there with our eyes wide open like little monkeys. Finally, one of the older children, brave enough, stepped forward and took a piece from the lady's hand, and that encouraged the rest of us to do the same.

The taste of that mysterious substance was magical. It was sweet with a hint of bitterness, and it just melted in our mouths without any effort. We had never seen, tasted, or heard of something like this before. It was a new and exciting flavor that none of us had ever experienced. Later in my life, I learned that this magical thing we tasted for the first time that day was dark chocolate.

While we were following this couple, there were many curious questions and eager discussions among us kids. We were wondering about their nature, questioning their skin, the strange clothes, and their unfamiliar features. "Are they made from plastic or something else?" one child wondered aloud, asking, "Do you think they shine in the dark since they're so bright now?"

A child in the back commented, "I bet they drink rainbows for breakfast!"

Driven by innocent curiosity, I finally asked a question that had been forming in my mind: "Do they go to the toilet the same way we do?"

In response, an older boy slapped the back of my head playfully and said, "And where do you think jam comes from?"

I looked into the other children's eyes, and it seemed like all agreed with his answer. For years after that playful exchange, I believed that white people were the main source of jam.

With the sunset, the couple walked towards one of the village houses. The owner, who had been waiting outside, greeted them warmly, and they entered his home. It was the end of our adventure, and everyone headed back to their respective homes.

The minute I entered my house, my father surprised me and slapped the blackness out of my face. Just at that moment I remembered I was supposed to buy supplies for lunch.

Continuing the memory, I recall how the experience with the white couple from my childhood replayed itself in a way but with roles reversed. In 2009 I decided to walk for a journey from Medan to Dumai in Sumatra Island in Indonesia, driven by a desire for fun, peace, and to enjoy the natural beauty of the environment. Every time I approached a village, and the children noticed me, they would run back to their homes screaming "Negroooo." Soon after, they would reemerge with their families and faces full of wonder—probably for many of them they had never seen a Black man in their entire lives.

As I walked, I became a curiosity, an unexpected event in their day. Children, sometimes adults as well, followed me for miles, their hands reaching out tentatively to touch my skin, their eyes wide and fascinated. I could see their imaginations spinning just as mine had when I saw that white couple.

On the first day of this trip, I felt annoyed by their actions, their shouts, and their stares. But then I remembered that white couple in my hometown. I remembered my own innocent curiosity, the thrill, and how graciously that couple had responded to our childish behaviors. They were understanding and kind; they gave us chocolate and smiles. Inspired by this memory, I immediately shifted my attitude. I did my best to respond with kindness and patience so they could build a nice memory of that day.

I discovered, too, the warmth of the Sumatran people. They welcomed me into their homes with open arms, generously offering food, shelter, rides, and companionship. In their eyes, I wasn't a foreigner or a stranger, but a guest—an honored visitor. They offered me beds to spend the night, and the meals we shared were filled with laughter and stories, bridges between our different worlds. Throughout my two weeks there, not once did I feel that they treated me differently due to the color of my skin.

Even when the children were screaming "Negroooo" I never felt offended or annoyed. I understood that their remark was coming from pure curiosity and surprise, not from racism or prejudice. To them, it was just a word—without the bitter weight it carries in other parts of the world. It was not a label.

On another occasion, I was in South Sudan for a humanitarian emergency response, and one of my colleagues was a woman from the UK. One day, after we finished our duties at one of the community centers in Rank City, she and I were discussing something by the side of the building. As we spoke, a little girl of about seven years old approached us.

With eyes wide and filled with curiosity, the girl looked up at me and asked in Arabic, "Uncle, is this white lady made of plastic?"

In a playful spirit, remembering my own childhood memories, I responded affirmatively. "Yes," I told her, playing along with her innocent wonder.

Her face lit up, a victory in her bright eyes. She turned and ran back to her group of friends, proclaiming, "I told you! She is made of plastic!"

My colleague, clearly puzzled by this sudden exchange, looked to me for an explanation. I translated the conversation for her and, seeing her initial shock, she quickly asked, "Why did you do that?" Then I shared my own story of the day I came to believe that white people were the magical source of jam and how that silly belief, once debunked, became a nice memory. Slowly, I could see my colleague's expression soften as she absorbed the story. Then she laughed and said, "It's funny how a simple interaction can turn into a story that lasts a lifetime."

ECHOES OF FATE

CHAPTER 8

The Dual Dance

I spend the weekend in a swirl of emotions, my heart teetering between excitement and anxiety. I am filled with hope and worry in equal measures, constantly thinking about the outcomes of the echo exam and what Dr. Andrzej's conclusion will be. Will he confirm the other doctors' diagnoses? Or will he offer me a different path, a chance to escape this situation and live a longer, healthier life?

Normally, I am skilled at wearing a poker face, rarely betraying my internal emotional state. I hardly ever look happy, sad, or worried. But this weekend is different; I am overwhelmed with feelings and emotions that bubble to the surface, despite my best efforts to keep them in check. It becomes so apparent that even my wife notices the change in me.

Seeing the concern etched across her face, I finally open up and explain the situation with Dr. Andrzej in detail. She listens intently. "Everything will be okay," she assures me. "We will be right there with you when you go to see Dr. Andrzej again, if you want us with you."

****

The three of us, my wife, my young son, and I, enter the doctor's office. Dr. Andrzej greets us warmly with a smile and asks us to take seats. My wife pulls a chair a little further behind me and sits with our son in her lap because he starts immediately touching and grabbing stuff from the doctor's desk.

This time, Dr. Andrzej makes an assumption when he speaks in Polish to my wife. He probably assumes from her appearance—white with dark red hair—that she is Polish. It seems like this is his way of finally satisfying his curiosity about why I am in Poland. Perhaps he is wondering if I am married to a Polish woman. However, he looks slightly disappointed when he realizes that she is American and does not speak Polish, which seems to make him even more curious. Despite this, he remains professional and doesn't inquire further.

He turns his attention back to me. He opens the sealed envelope and reads the report. He then grows serious. "I am reviewing your echo cardiogram in detail," he starts in English, clearly aware of my wife's presence and ensuring she understands. As he continues to explain, I feel my heart race, but I intently focus on Dr. Andrzej's words, bracing myself for what comes next.

"Your heart condition isn't promising, and its performance is very weak. You likely have until next January," he informs me. So far, he tells me nothing I don't already know. He leans back in his chair, pausing for a long moment, then fixes a serious gaze on me. "But I may be able to fix it," he says. Before I even have a chance to react, he adds, "Don't get your hopes up. It's going to be a complicated intervention, and the chance of success stands at only 50%."

Out of my happiness and ignorance, I immediately respond, "50%? That's great—others gave me 0% chances."

He cuts me off and says, "No, 50% is not good. The minimum success threshold that we surgeons accept is 93% and above." He continues, "I am planning to try something new—let's call it an experiment. If it works, I can guarantee you'll live for at least 30 more years. If it doesn't work, it doesn't make a difference; you're dead anyway."

Before he can ask me what I think about his suggestion, I interrupt and say, "Let's do it."

Both my wife and the doctor are in shock because of my quick response and decisive reaction. Dr. Andrzej tries to persuade me to go home, think about it, and discuss it with my wife. Then we can discuss what we will do and the implications of the intervention further.

Here is something that neither the doctor nor my wife knows. For the last two months, all the doctors from different parts of the world have given me the same grim prognosis—I am going to die very soon—and that includes Dr. Andrzej. However, Dr. Andrzej is the only one out of all of them who has given me even a sliver of hope. Of course, I'll take that percentage, even if it is only 5%, never mind 50%. That is a no-brainer, just a simple math calculation and a realistic decision based on stark facts. I don't want other people's—even my wife's—feelings and concerns to influence this moment of my life.

I respond politely, "No, no need for all that. I am ready to take my chances, so let's do it."

He begins to explain the process and the procedures and what will happen next. I am not really paying attention to most of what he is saying. My wife is interacting with him and asking questions, but I am in my own imaginary world of happiness, until he asks suddenly, "Do you have any infection in your body?" He continues, "Any kind of infection needs to be treated before we do this surgery; otherwise, it will fail."

I am about to say no, I don't have any infection, when suddenly I remember something. Three years ago, while I was in Afghanistan, I developed a small papilla, a bump on the skin of my butt. It would disappear for some time but kept coming back. The doctor in the German clinic in Kabul told me that it was a fistula and might require minor surgery to be removed. Then I learnt the fistula is an abnormal connection between two body parts generally caused by an injury, surgery, infection, or inflammation.

However, my doctor in Italy insisted that it was not a fistula but a simple papilla and that it would eventually go away. He refused to refer me to a specialist. One of the great aspects of living in Italy is the free healthcare service for nationals and legal residents, which is awesome. However, one of the downsides is that the private healthcare sector has been weakened. Therefore, I could not bypass my primary doctor to consult with someone else about the papilla and seek treatment.

When Dr. Andrzej hears this story, he says, "If that is a fistula, it is definitely the reason behind your recent heart symptoms, and it needs to be treated before we proceed with our surgery." Then he explains how dangerous any type of infection can be for someone with a heart condition like mine, even if it's a small fistula. At the end he scribbles something on a piece of paper and hands it to me. "This is the contact of one of the best fistula surgeons in Poland. I'll let her know, and you should go and see her immediately," he instructs, concluding with, "Don't come back until you've treated that."

As we leave the office, I put aside the possible infection and am filled with a profound sense of joy and hope because of this new development. My wife, on the other hand, carries a look of worry on her face due to the 50% success rate of the surgery. And my son, tired from the day, just wants to sleep. It's a moment that captures the different emotional worlds we each inhabit, even though we are moving through this experience together as a family.

****

In Arabic, there is a saying, "Problems don't come singly." It feels as though this phrase has taken on a life of its own in my world. It's as if the universe is playing a cruel game with me, stacking the deck when I am already on my knees. I am already in the fight of my life, grappling with my own mortality, battling to retain hope in the face of hopeless medical predictions, and now another issue rears its head, demanding immediate attention before I can even think of returning to Dr. Andrzej.

As if my heart condition weren't enough, now this persisting fistula, which had been a mere discomfort before, has suddenly become a critical issue I need to clear. I feel like a boxer who has already taken a severe beating, only to be surprised by the referee allowing another round. The weariness is bone-deep; it's not just physical exhaustion but an emotional and mental fatigue that's hard to put into words. It's the kind of tired that sleep doesn't cure.

My mind begins to think about the logistics. Will treating the fistula delay my heart surgery too much? What if an infection from this minor surgery complicates the major one? I have many other questions that I cannot answer.

The absurdity of it all almost makes me laugh. It's like a tragic comedy; every time we think we've scaled a mountain, we find another, taller facing us. I was so focused on my heart, so consumed by the looming, intricate surgery, that I almost forgot about the rest of my body. It seems ridiculous that something as small as a bump on my ass could become a deciding factor in my survival.

But in this moment, amid frustration and fear, I dig deep within myself and find a stubborn ember of resilience that refuses to be extinguished—I will survive.

As I prepare for this unexpected turn, I am strengthening and assuring myself: I will take on this new challenge as I have faced others—with determination, grace, and the love of my family as my guiding light. Problems may not come singly, but neither do the resources with which I can use to fight them. My resolve, the love of my family, and a medical team willing to take a chance on me—they're my arsenal. With them, I'm ready to fight.

ASSIM SALIH

The surgeon recommended by Dr. Andrzej confirms what the doctor at the German clinic in Kabul had previously diagnosed: it's a fistula and it needs to be removed urgently if I have any hopes of living a longer life. And of course, I want that chance.

However, a new problem presents itself. All the private hospitals in Warsaw are hesitant to allow the procedure on their properties. Their reservations come from my existing heart condition. The anesthesia required for the surgery could complicate the matter, potentially resulting in fatal consequences. For them, it's a liability too great to take, a high risk they're unwilling to embark upon. This leaves us with one alternative: the public hospitals in Poland.

One night, after returning from Iraq, I found myself channel-surfing the TV. I stumbled upon a comedy show set in a Polish public hospital. It was like the famous TV show "House M.D." but this series was set in a Polish environment and was even funnier. The stories revolved around the chaos within that hospital: a doctor who attempts to perform surgeries while intoxicated, rats running through the wards, surgeries being performed on the wrong patients, frequent clashes between nurses and patients, and so on.

The show aired nightly from 11 p.m. to midnight. Although it was in Polish—a language I don't speak—I found myself able to understand the comedic situations clearly through the actors' expressive performances. Each night, after an episode finished, I prayed that I would never have to set foot in a public hospital in Warsaw, even though I recognized that is just a TV show and might not be an actual reflection of reality.

The TV show brings back vivid memories of hospitals in Sudan, with their own brand of chaos and confusion. Instead of rats, it's cats that roam the halls. They move around from one ward to another with authority, as if they are part of the senior medical staff. One thing always strikes me: despite the conditions of the hospitals, the cats always appear in excellent health. I've sometimes thought, with grim humor, that perhaps these cats are nourished on whatever they can find in the morgue.

Back in the day when I was at the university in Sudan, one of our colleagues felt unbearable stomach pain. His friends rushed him to the hospital, where the doctor informed them that his appendix was infected and needed to be removed immediately. After the procedure, with the appendix successfully removed, the hospital staff asked his friends to carry him on a stretcher to the ward on the second floor because there is no elevator in the hospital.

Four of them carried the stretcher, with our colleague still unconscious from the anesthesia. He was a bit overweight, and they struggled climbing the stairs. At the last step before reaching the second floor, they lost control and dropped him. He rolled down the stairs all the way to the ground floor, and, because he was under anesthesia, his legs and arms were flailing everywhere; he broke all four.

The doctors administered more anesthesia and put his arms and legs in casts. A few hours later, he regained consciousness to find himself swaddled in plaster and pain in his entire body. He managed to open his eyes and asked his friend in disbelief, "Remind me again, what kind of surgery did they say I was getting?"

So, when the surgeon brings up the option of a public hospital, I couldn't help but laugh and share both the TV show anecdotes and the story of my colleague. She laughs along with me and assures me that everything will be all right. She promises that there is a reputable public hospital where she has connections, and she will try to persuade the administration to allow us to conduct the procedure there. True to her word, she succeeds.

I am scheduled for the fistula surgery on Wednesday, November 23, 2016, at 3:00 p.m., but I must arrive at the hospital three hours in advance for preparation and plan on being there for the night. The surgeon confirms that a skilled cardiologist will be on standby in the hospital, and, in case of any complications, he will be ready to intervene. If necessary, I would be swiftly transferred to the cardiology section within the same hospital. On the other hand, Dr. Andrzej emphasizes that in case of a cardiac emergency, an ambulance must immediately transport me to Medicover Hospital in Warsaw, where he could take charge of my care.

It seems that everything has been meticulously arranged for that Wednesday; all that remains is for me to be psychologically prepared. In truth, I'm not particularly worried about the surgery itself. Instead, my anxiety stems from the potential train wreck that I might experience in this local hospital, given the chaotic scenarios that I've heard and imagined about such settings.

We arrive at the hospital three hours in advance, as instructed. The scene that greets us is all too familiar, and I can't help but be reminded of the TV show. The main entrance door to the hospital is propped open with a large ashtray. Medical staff and patients alike are smoking, with a significant amount of smoke drifting into the hospital corridor. The floor is old, worn-out vinyl, and the paint on the walls is faded and inconsistent. Uniforms seem to be optional here; each staff member is dressed differently, sporting a variety of colors and styles. I can hardly differentiate the doctors from the nurses from the cleaners.

The hospital bed designated for me looks ancient, likely a survivor from the Second World War. I can't help but wonder how many soldiers might have breathed their last on this very bed. While I haven't spotted any rats as of yet, I tell myself that perhaps they're on the night shift. But my biggest challenge? The language barrier. No one seems to understand or speak English. Thank goodness for my friend, Ali, who's there to act as my translator and bridge the gap.

As a patient, I've become something of an expert in hospital procedures and surgeries. I know exactly how to prepare for this surgery from the comfort of my home. Due to the location of the fistula, it's necessary to shave both my front and back private areas. I'd rather not have a nurse handling and moving my penis left and right to shave the hair—I've been in that situation before, and it was exceedingly awkward. Furthermore, in case of heart complications, they might need to insert some tubes into my neck, necessitating a clean-shaven face. And who knows? If things take a turn for the worse, they might have to open my chest, which means that too would have to be shaved. So, this morning, I spent an hour in the bathroom, meticulously shaving every hair off my body, including my head. Afterward, I took a refreshing shower and doused myself with antiseptic alcohol.

A nurse, round-shaped and probably in her late 40s, who looks more like a kitchen cleaner than a medical professional, asks me to follow her to the preparation room. The room is of a decent size, with a high bed situated in the center, a table with a shaving machine on top. In the back right corner, there's a showerhead and a drain on the floor but no curtains. Near the door is a chair with a towel, slippers, and a blue patient gown on top.

She closes the door behind us and instructs me to undress, leaving me standing in just my underwear. Pointing for me to lie on the bed, she puts on a pair of gloves and assists in removing my underwear. Noticing the smooth shaving of my body, she appears surprised. However, she still performs a check by adjusting my penis left and right. She then lifts a thumb in approval, commending in English, "Good, good."

She then indicates for me to shower using a soap with a strong antiseptic aroma. What's bizarre is her decision to remain in the room, seated just a few feet away, as I wash. She watches intently, occasionally pointing out areas she believes I missed, urging me to lather and rinse repeatedly. I can't help but wonder if she mistakenly believes my skin color is some sort of dirt or stain. But after an extensive 15 minutes of washing, she seems to give up on whitening my color. Drying off with the provided towel, I slide into the slippers and put on the gown, which unfortunately does little to cover my backside. I return to my room after flashing everyone in the corridor with my smooth and freshly shaved black ass.

Now I understand how the surgeon managed to persuade the hospital administration to let us perform the surgery in their facility. She enters the room with a group of medical students trailing behind her and asks if I would mind them attending the surgery as well.

Back in high school, my favorite subjects were math, biology, physics, and chemistry. I used to read about these subjects for fun, while most of my peers despised them. During my university years, I lived with some medical students for a few months. One night, I overheard them complaining about the difficulty of their biology curriculum. They couldn't understand a particular topic, so I offered to have a look. They handed me the book mockingly—I was not a medical student, after all. Reading a few pages, I found the content—relating to hormone functionality and chemical changes during the menstrual cycle—quite straightforward. I explained it to them, simplifying the concepts, and they appreciated my perspective. From that point on, I began studying with them just for fun.

As I worked with them, I noticed that much of the material, particularly concerning dermatology and diseases with skin symptoms, seemed tailored to patients with lighter skin tones. The descriptions and diagnoses referenced pink reddish skin, skin turning blue, how eyes perceive vein colors, and so on. I have never seen my skin turning pink or blue. This revelation made me empathize with darker-skinned patients, as I realized that this bias in medical education could affect their care. Perhaps this is the reason why my doctor back in Italy couldn't diagnose my fistula years ago. It's possible that he couldn't see any red or pink color on my skin because he was accustomed only to treating patients with white skin. Bless him for assuming everyone comes in just one shade!

When the surgeon asked for my permission to allow the students to observe the surgery, I was initially inclined to say no. But then, I considered that this might be a golden opportunity for these aspiring doctors to learn how to locate and remove a fistula without relying on skin color indication—a kind of hands-on, blindfolded bicycle ride, so to speak.

With my agreement, she starts detailing the procedures. It will involve local anesthesia and is expected to take about 45 minutes, and I should be able to leave the hospital the following morning. However, she warns that due to my heart condition, I might feel dizzy during the procedure. If this were to happen, I should notify them immediately, as this could signal a potential heart-related risk and require urgent cardiologist involvement.

I am there in the operating room, feeling the cuts, the pulls, and the scrapes, but no pain, until they successfully finish without any complications. They move me to the intensive care unit, and a minute after that, the monitor I am connected to starts beeping, and I begin to feel very dizzy.

Immediately, I know that my heart is acting up—I am in grave danger. The surgeon rushes to me and tries her best, screaming, "Stay with me Assim, stay with me," while waiting for the cardiologist. For about an hour, I hover between consciousness and unconsciousness, until my condition stabilizes a bit and the monitor stops beeping. Then she assures me that the cardiologist is on his way and leaves.

I am in that hospital for almost two days waiting for the cardiologist, who never shows up. My heart condition worsens by the hour, the machine beeps every few minutes, I am constantly fading in and out of consciousness, but no one seems to care—it's like a scene straight out of that TV comedy show. I request to be transferred to Medicover Hospital immediately as Dr. Andrzej recommended, but the doctors in the hospital tell me they can't do that unless the cardiologist orders it.

I think they might not understand my English, so I ask my wife and, when he comes to visit me, Ali, to translate to them my concerns and desires to be transferred to the other hospital. Still, the outcome remains the same: I can't be transferred without the cardiologist's order. Then I request to be discharged, but they refuse that as well.

Finally, I have to take matters into my own hands and tell the doctor that if the cardiologist does not show up in the next hour, I am walking out of this hospital no matter what, threatening to call a taxi to Medicover Hospital.

Another hour passes, and the cardiologist still doesn't show up. I insist on leaving the hospital. The doctor has me sign a liability discharge paper, and my wife and I take a taxi to Medicover where Dr. Andrzej is waiting for us.

****

The presence of a special person can provide significant emotional comfort to someone who is unwell. This emotional support can help alleviate the feelings of stress, anxiety, and isolation that often accompany illness. Being with someone meaningful can also act as a distraction, shifting the patient's focus from their discomfort or pain to a concern about how the loved one is feeling.

Physiologically, spending time with a dear individual can trigger the release of endorphins, the body's natural painkillers and mood enhancers, potentially reducing perceived pain and elevating feelings of wellbeing. Physical touch, such as hugging or holding hands, can be therapeutic, leading to a lower heart rate, reduced blood pressure, and decreased levels of stress hormones.

The power of emotional and social support extends to potentially boosting the immune system, as loneliness and chronic stress can suppress immune responses. Positive social interactions can have the opposite effect, enhancing immune function. Additionally, the placebo effect might come into play; if a sick individual believes that a special person's presence will help them feel better, this belief alone can contribute to an improved sense of wellbeing. Ultimately, while emotional and social support isn't a substitute for medical care, it plays a significant and beneficial role in healing and recovery.

In my case, that special individual is Dr. Andrzej.

****

I'm not feeling well in the taxi ride from the public hospital to Medicover Hospital, and I feel like I might collapse. Despite this, I push my limits to stay awake and manage to walk straight when I arrive at Medicover. After finalizing the paperwork at the reception, they escort me to my room in a wheelchair. A few minutes later, Dr. Andrzej knocks and enters the room, accompanied by another doctor.

I've met Dr. Andrzej only twice, but it feels like we've known each other forever. His presence immediately eases my discomfort; the dizziness subsides, the stress and anxiety dissipate. I can breathe easier, I find myself smiling, and I detect the scent of cigar on his clothes. From being unable to walk and feeling completely drained, suddenly I am rejuvenated.

He greets me warmly, as usual, and introduces the other doctor—the head of the cardiology department at the hospital and one of his best students. He reassures me with a comforting phrase: "Don't worry, you are in safe hands now."

In the blink of an eye, the room transforms into a hive of activity. Nurses, moving with the urgency that my situation demands but without any sense of panic, rush around me. They are hooking me up to machines and monitors that immediately start charting the rhythm and nuances of my heart and vitals. An oxygen mask is gently placed over my face, a thin tube inserted smoothly into my vein, and IV drips are started that infuse both medications and fluids to stabilize my condition.

In the middle of this bustle, another doctor is beside me, running through a list of detailed questions about my medical history, recent activities, and current symptoms. She's typing down my responses on a digital pad, her face a picture of deep concentration. It's clear she knows what she's doing, her questions insightful, and her manner professional.

From the corner of the room, Dr. Andrzej and the head of the cardiology department are overseeing the situation. Their experienced eyes are constantly scanning, assessing, and directing. The atmosphere they create is one of calm control. Dr. Andrzej and his colleague occasionally give some instructions, their tones steady and assuring. Each command causes a nurse to perform a new task.

I catch Dr. Andrzej's eye for a moment, and he gives me a reassuring nod, reinforcing his earlier promise. In that brief connection, an overwhelming sense of relief washes over me. I feel that I've made the right decision, acting as my own advocate, and discharging myself from that public hospital. I might have been just another tragic tale on that TV comedy show otherwise.

ASSIM SALIH

As I am lying back on the bed and begin to feel the sedative effects of the medication, I can't help but reflect on the stark contrast between this environment and my previous experience in the public hospital. With that thought, and under the watchful eyes of Dr. Andrzej and his team, I allow myself to relax for the first time in what feels like an eternity, confident that I am, indeed, in the very best of hands.

ECHOES OF FATE

CHAPTER 9

The Fake Color

The following morning, as the nurse wakes me to draw some blood, I notice how spacious my room is compared to the one at the other hospital. The room is a generous size with walls in white with hints of grey, my favorite colors. The modern and comfortable hospital bed is adjustable with a wireless remote control on the stylish nightstand beside me. I have my own bathroom, so I don't need to walk in the corridor and potentially flash anyone. A 42-inch TV hangs on the wall in front of me. To my right, a window opens to the back of the hospital, offering a lovely view of a small garden. To the left of the bed, about five feet away, two armchairs sit with a tea table between them. On the wall above the chairs, a beautiful painting of horses running in a green field. Next to the bathroom door stands a large wooden closet where my clothes and belongings could be stored.

A hospital staff member brings me breakfast: a boiled egg sliced atop some salad, a few cutlets, yogurt, and a cup of coffee. Even though I'm not usually a breakfast person, I clear the tray, savoring every bite, and enjoy my coffee as I watch the news.

It's funny how simple things can make me so happy. In this room, I feel like I'm on vacation at a luxurious resort, not sick at a hospital. There's an odd sense of comfort here, so profound that I could imagine happily staying in this place for the rest of my life, which, given my current health condition, may not be that long.

I think part of my joy in this room is also due to the fact that I am a minimalist by nature, though not in the same way as those who consciously choose minimalism as a lifestyle and philosophy. For me, physical possessions simply don't hold much meaning or value. It is not about adhering to a particular creed or movement but rather a natural inclination I have always felt. My possessions are utilitarian and limited only to the essentials, reflecting a practical and uncomplicated approach to life. Everything I have in this world can fit in one bag, weighing no more than 50 pounds. Additionally, I place little emphasis on occasions like birthdays, Father's Day, or other similar celebrations. To me, these so-called "special" days don't hold much significance. In fact, I have a distinct aversion to receiving gifts. I am a firm believer in the idea that if I want something, I will buy it myself. If I haven't bought it, that likely means I don't need it.

Also, I'm someone who doesn't necessarily find peace or rejuvenation from being in nature. The rustling of leaves, the scent of pine, and the colors and smells of autumn don't particularly uplift me. While I appreciate these experiences when they occur, I don't actively seek them out or feel a sense of loss without them. For me, life encompasses more significant concerns that demand my attention and thought, far beyond feeling rejuvenated by a walk in nature or hiking mountains.

In this modern, clean, and peaceful room, with its tasteful décor and technology at my fingertips, I feel content. I can reach out to friends and family, watch the latest news, or lose myself in a book or movie. It's remarkable how such a seemingly small comfort can cast a warm, reassuring light on everything, even though I'm in a place most people wouldn't associate with relaxation and happiness.

In Norway, while a friend was driving me around, I noticed a facility surrounded by a 3-foot-high fence. Beyond it lay a big green yard, where people walked around wearing the same uniforms. It looked like a military camp, so I asked my friend what it was. To my surprise, she told me it was a prison. I was taken aback; how could a prison be fenced with only a 3-foot-high fence? It seemed unthinkable compared to the imposing prison barriers I was accustomed to.

To satisfy my curiosity, I looked deeper into the correctional system in Norway, and what I discovered was incredible. God forbid, but if I were sent to a Norwegian prison it wouldn't feel like a punishment or taking away my freedom but more like a transformative retreat—a place for education and reflection. In fact, and I'm not kidding, spending a couple of years in a Norwegian prison seems like it would be 10 times more pleasant than spending them in Sudan. I mean, who wouldn't trade the desert heat and tough life for a cozy Nordic cell with a window view?

Personally, I don't understand people who feel suffocated and burned out if they don't get to step outside, change their scenery, or breathe some fresh air. For me, these activities are a luxury, not a necessity. I've observed this restlessness directly during our humanitarian response missions. When curfews were imposed and our time outside the compounds was restricted, some people just started to breakdown. They grew increasingly restless, got sick physically and mentally, counting down the days until they could leave for a vacation.

A friend of mine, assigned to Juba in South Sudan, struggled significantly with their strict curfews and limited social interactions, compounded by a lack of connection with nature. This environment led to her experiencing stress, restlessness, and physical symptoms like hair loss. Such challenges highlight that humanitarian missions aren't for everyone; they require strength, resilience, and empathy. The hardships aid workers think they face, though real, often pale in comparison to the local people's experiences. It's important for those in such roles in the humanitarian sector to maintain perspective and appreciate their relative fortune, focusing on the deeper plight of the local community. Otherwise, they're clearly in the wrong line of work.

I know that I sound harsh, strict, and judgmental, but life has been an effective teacher in this respect. It has shown me the contrasts in people's resilience and perspective, and I retain and value these lessons.

****

In the afternoon, Ali and a group of other Sudanese friends and acquaintances arrive at the hospital to pay me a visit—all 17 of them at the same time! The hospital staff, in a state of mild shock, quickly decides that only five visitors at a time can see me in order to prevent any disturbance for the other patients. They bring with them authentic

Sudanese food, fruits, candies, and flowers. The amusing part? I don't even recognize more than half of these people.

Let me tell you a bit about Sudanese culture. Visiting the sick, whether at home or in the hospital, is deeply rooted in Sudanese culture, as it represents a social, religious, and moral duty that exceeds family ties. It is considered an act of sympathy and solidarity that emphasizes the interdependence of Sudanese society. When someone falls ill and is admitted to a hospital, it is common for relatives, friends, colleagues, and others to visit them, not only on the first day but also throughout the patient's stay. Despite the frequency of visits, the hospital visiting hours and the patient's condition are usually respected. If the visitors come to the hospital outside of the designated visiting hours, they often settle in the hospital yard for hours. They generously bring food, snacks, as well as hot and cold beverages, not just for the patient but also for other patients, their relatives, and anyone else waiting at the hospital for their loved ones.

In general, the Sudanese are famous for their warmth and kindness. Welcoming guests and treating them with the utmost respect is firmly embedded in the culture. If you visit any Sudanese home, you are likely to get a feast, even if the family doesn't have much. Sharing what one owns, even if it is just a little bit, is an established value. Also, it is common for Sudanese to invite strangers into their homes for meals. This open heart is a testament to their generosity.

In February 2003, I decided to visit my hometown for just a few of days after being away for quite some time. By that point, my family had already moved away from Darfur and settled in another part of Sudan. I knew almost everyone in the town, so I was concerned about where to stay during my visit. There were no hotels or accommodation that I could rent, and choosing to stay with my one friend might create issues with others who might feel slighted that I didn't choose their home. Nevertheless, I decided to proceed with my travels and would figure out my accommodations once I arrived.

Just before boarding a bus, I met someone whose younger brother I had studied with in high school. We chatted for a bit, and he wished me a safe journey. Several hours later, as the bus entered my hometown, I asked the driver to let me off at the stop in our old neighborhood. However, the driver replied seriously, "I have been told to only let you off at the bus station." When I inquired further, he maintained his seriousness and said, "You will find out when we get there, so please return to your seat." I sat down, worried about who had made this request. Given the political tension in Darfur at the time and considering that a few of my high school colleagues had launched a military campaign against the government, I feared that the government's security service might be involved, wanting to question my reasons for returning at such a tense political time.

To my surprise, when we arrived at the bus station, the entire family of the guy I had met before boarding the bus was waiting for me. He had conveyed the news to his older brothers that I was arriving, and they had decided to host me at their home. As they greeted me, other people recognized me, and everyone was pulling me towards them, insisting that I stay with them. In that moment, someone I recognized from high school picked up my duffle bag, shouting over the noise of the crowd, "I don't care where you will be staying, but this bag is going to our home!" and he took off. At the end, I stayed where my duffle bag had been taken.

For the three days I was there, I was treated with overwhelming generosity. I was given a car with a full tank of gas to move around the town. Everyone I met and every house I visited invited me for a meal. Older people tried to give me money, even though I explained that I was employed and had a good salary—and that they needed the money more than I did. Some even got upset and insisted I take the money. I was not allowed to pay for anything. When I wanted to buy a pack of cigarettes, I was given an entire carton for free. Even my return bus tickets were paid for, and I still don't know by whom. That is how extensive the generosity and hospitality of the people back home is.

On a beautiful sunny morning in the summer of 2014, by the sea in Alghero on Sardinia Island, I met a Jehovah's Witness couple. Their question about my faith in Jesus led to my spontaneous invitation: "If you want to know, meet me here at this same spot at 6 p.m.; I'll take you to my place for dinner, then we can discuss." They were shocked and confused, but they accepted my invitation.

Living alone at the time, their acceptance filled me with joy. In anticipation, I prepared for the evening with shopping and cooking, even inviting my neighbor to join our dinner. At 6 p.m., I was back at the spot, and the couple, Jan and Anna, arrived shortly after, having decided to trust my invitation. During our walk to my place, sensing their hesitation and concerns, I candidly reassured them, saying, "Don't worry, I'm not going to kidnap or harm you. It's just dinner, and then we'll each go our own way." This straightforward assurance was meant to ease their concerns and make them comfortable.

That evening at my home, we shared a delightful dinner and engaged in deep conversations about life, science, and mostly about the spontaneous invitation and Sudanese. Jan, from Sweden, and Anna, from the Czech Republic, shared about their lives, children. and their business in Corsica.

Because of their inquiry about my belief in Jesus, we remained in touch up to today, and I even visited them in Corsica. That spontaneous invitation resulted a long-lasting friendship driven by my inherent Sudanese values of openness and hospitality.

Furthermore, Sudanese culture places a high value on honesty and trust, which are deeply rooted in the society. For many Sudanese, one's word is one's bond, and trustworthiness is an integral part of everyday interactions. For instance, in 2013, while my wife and I were traveling from Afghanistan to Italy, a family emergency required me to send money urgently to Sudan. Despite being in transit, I managed to find a solution at the Dubai airport. I approached a random Sudanese traveler bound for Khartoum, explained to him the emergency situation, and entrusted him with $2,500 USD to deliver to my brother who would be waiting for him at the airport in Sudan.

Throughout our flight to Milan, my wife was skeptical and convinced that we had lost the money. However, to her astonishment, upon our arrival in Milan, I received a text message from my brother confirming he had received the money. This act of trust, which might seem extraordinary in other parts of the world, is not uncommon in Sudanese culture—a fact that left a lasting impression on my wife, who remarked that such a gesture would be unthinkable in the United States.

****

In the evening, following the visits from my Sudanese friends and family, the surgeon who had performed the fistula surgery at the public hospital paid me a surprise visit. She came to check on my condition, change the dressing, and see how I was recovering. She expressed deep apologies about the situation at the hospital and admitted that she had felt let down by the cardiologist's actions. I understood it wasn't her fault, and in fact, I truly appreciated her efforts.

I turn on the TV to see what is going on in the world. Still the looming Trump presidency dominates the news until I catch the sports segment. Andy Murray had secured the year-end number one ranking in tennis, regular matches were taking place in the European football leagues, the Autumn Internationals in rugby had concluded, the NFL was in the midst of its regular season, and Nico Rosberg had won the World Championship in a closely fought contest with his teammate, Lewis Hamilton.

When I hear about Lewis Hamilton, I suddenly start feeling tightness in my chest, my heartbeat is becoming rapid, and I am beginning to feel nauseous. Anger and resentment surface, a mix of feelings and emotions boiling in my veins. I become very angry and feel like breaking things. My hands are shaking, and my heart is racing. I want to let out my anger on everything around me, destroying whatever is in the room—letting it all out. Damn you Orderud!

After the loss of my childhood friend, Sabir, it was hard for me to open up to anyone else until I crossed paths with Orderud during one of my missions. Right from the start, we had a connection. Orderud showed maturity, open-mindedness, honesty, and genuine feeling. More importantly, the relationship provided me with a safe space to empty some of the weight I had been carrying. I entrusted Orderud with my life, and always listened with genuine interest and compassion. It felt like I had found another Sabir in my life, someone truly special.

While we shared many common interests, we also had our differences, which we respected and embraced. These differences enriched our bond and provided a balance in our interactions. Orderud loved mountaineering and had a genuine passion for nature, always seeking the thrill of a new adventure. Despite my general indifference towards nature, I had always harbored a desire to join in on Orderud's adventures, but I never managed to do so.

Everything seemed harmonious, until one day Orderud became distant, citing purely selfish and egotistic reasons before disappearing forever. This sudden turn was heart wrenching, a depth of disappointment words could not capture. I felt anger, sadness, shock, and confusion. I never expected betrayal, especially not from the one person I thought would never deceive me.

The world felt contaminated with memories of Orderud, making it challenging for me to enjoy anything without a painful memory: the songs that we used to like, the cars that we used to dream of, the mountains Orderud loved, the TV shows that we used to watch, and our mutual admiration for Usain Bolt and Lewis Hamilton.

I had believed Orderud was my new Sabir. But while Sabir stood by me till his last moments in the most difficult circumstances, Orderud chose a different path simply because of a new opportunity and better social status. I was left behind in my most needed moment, leaving me feeling both betrayed and misled.

For years, I wrestled with intense emotions, held even dark feelings, and wished Orderud would suffer. However, I continually reminded myself to rise above, to be the better person. The world is full of people like Orderud, and it's nearly impossible to find a faithful friend like Sabir. But I learned my lesson and I have been more guarded since then.

In the journey of life, we often encounter individuals who pretend to be sincere and genuine; in fact, some of them may not even know the dark side of themselves. Such people are numerous, and it seems almost impossible to avoid them. We could easily be fooled and deceived by their disguised facades, thinking they are true allies, only to eventually have them unveil their true colors. The realization can be heartbreaking, even toxic, leaving us feeling betrayed and questioning our judgment. The experience of such betrayals is intense, which makes us wonder how we didn't see their true nature earlier. However, as inevitable as these experiences seem, all we can do is accept the pain and move on. However, some scars remain as very deep reminders that are not easily forgotten.

Finally, I turn off the TV and try to focus on the beeping sound coming from the heart monitor that I'm connected to. I lie back with my eyes closed, saying, "You'd better sleep. Orderud doesn't deserve a second of your remaining life." I drift off to sleep.

CHAPTER 10

Navigating Worlds Apart

I am still at Medicover Hospital, and it's been 48 hours. I feel better. The head of the cardiology department is entering my room. After we exchange greetings and asks about my wellbeing, he is checking my file and reading the notes from other doctors. With his eyes still glued to the file, he comments, "Good, very good." Pulling up an armchair, he sits beside me. "I'm so glad you saved yourself by coming here on time. A little delay and you'd be in a different situation." He is explaining my current state of health and the treatment I am undergoing. He expresses satisfaction that I am under Dr. Andrzej's care and emphasizes that he is the best they know. "You aren't in danger anymore and are showing significant improvement. I'm having the doctors remove the monitors to make you more comfortable," he tells me. "But to be on the safe side, I suggest you stay with us for a few more days and wear a mobile monitor. I want to ensure you're 100% okay before we discharge you."

ECHOES OF FATE

I am pleased with the doctor's recommendation to extend my hospital stay for a few additional days. Over the last 48 hours, amidst receiving the necessary care and medications, I've come to appreciate the opportunity to rest without the pressure of medical appointments or tending to my family's needs. Having struggled to get a good night's sleep for weeks, the hospital environment provides a sense of reassurance; hooked up to monitoring devices, I can rest assured that any irregularities will prompt immediate attention from the staff. While I've had a few visitors, mostly family and Sudanese friends, the greatest joy comes from spending time with my sons. Their presence brings me immense happiness, and I cherish the moments we share, relishing their innocent inquiries and expressions of wonder. At times, I've found myself contemplating life and considering the changes I would make if given another chance. Through these reflections, I've gained a deeper sense of peace and acceptance regarding whatever the future may hold. Surprisingly, the atmosphere of the hospital room has brought a welcome sense of relaxation and clarity to my thoughts.

Shortly after the discussion, the doctor leaves, delivering the good news that my condition has improved. A nurse arrives, quickly removing all the wires and equipment. After her, another doctor enters carrying a small device, roughly the size of a mobile phone. She proceeds to attach its wires to my chest and instructs me to wear the device around my neck continuously. With a nod, she mentions that I am now free to move about the hospital, and I was excited to walk around.

After returning from my walk, I sit down for lunch. Lounging on the armchair, I wonder whether to nap or watch a film on my laptop. The TV offers nothing but the boring news about Trump's presidency. Out of the blue, a memory strikes me, and I find myself smiling, then laughing. It takes me back to the first time I ever watched something on TV.

Back in the day, although many homes in Darfur had TVs, my hometown lacked both electricity and a signal. These televisions were always displayed as predominately as possible, not for use but as a symbol of prestige and hope for a future. The TVs were considered expensive possessions and were meticulously maintained, always clean and dust-free. Us children were strictly forbidden from even getting near them.

I hadn't seen a functioning TV until I was in the first grade. That was when a non-profit organization made its way to our town. I was too young to understand their reason for being in town, but I recall they used a house in our neighborhood as a residence, and one evening they invited the entire neighborhood for a film.

A 24-inch TV was strategically placed in the center of the yard, connected to a DVR, and powered by a car battery. Every child and woman from the neighborhood were present, but only a handful of men. We children sat on the ground just a few feet from the screen, while the adults were in the back sitting on benches, chairs, and water containers. Some were standing. As the movie started, there was an immediate stir of astonishment among us. The colors, people, cars, buildings, streets, and sounds fascinated us. The images were so captivating. We kids were so curious and kept moving closer to the screen, especially when the camera shifted away from something interesting. Then we were asked to sit back and remain quiet so everyone could enjoy the experience.

The film was an action movie featuring Bruce Lee, and every scene held our attention; we engaged with excitement. Laughter erupted during comedic moments, screams filled the air during tense scenes, and the audience interacted enthusiastically with the characters. Shouts of "Look behind, he's coming for you!" and "Don't let him escape!" were interspersed with curious queries like "What's that they're eating? It looks delicious!" The atmosphere was electric with participation and excitement.

It was an unforgettable evening. Once the movie ended, everyone was out in the street for hours recounting their favorite scenes, debating interpretations even though no one understood the language, and sharing laughter deep into the night. Meanwhile, we children playfully mimicked the fight sequences we had seen and chased each other around.

The next day, our conversations were entirely around the film, as we recounted our favorite parts. By the evening, we got even more excited as we were invited for another movie night. The crowd this time was twice as large, with more men in attendance and newcomers from neighboring areas. We children felt like experts on where to sit and how to behave. Some children almost started a fight because they wanted to sit in the front row, but an older lady intervened and brought order. All eyes were wide open and focused on the screen. Everyone waited for the film to begin.

A few minutes into the movie, chaos broke out. All of a sudden, the children, including myself, began screaming and rushing out of the yard, and several adults followed. Those who hadn't seen the previous movie stood confused by the chaos and didn't know what was going on. Some started running without even knowing why. It was almost comical to see some people join in the panic without having seen what caused it. But we all quickly regrouped, our faces a mixture of fear and confusion. The volunteers of the non-profit organization looked surprised, unable to understand the situation. They sent one of them to check with us.

In the movie we watched the night before, one of the bad guys had been killed at the end of the movie. When this second movie started, that very same guy who had been killed in the previous movie was playing a role in this very movie. We thought he must be a ghost because we all witnessed him dying last evening.

Because of our ignorance we thought everything in the movies was real life; we did not know anything about acting or casting. We thought when someone dies in a movie, they should remain dead and not appear in another movie. Eventually some of us crept back hesitantly to continue watching. Even after the volunteers explained how movies work, many did not believe them and refused to go back.

****

Our lives back in my hometown were rooted in simplicity, and our aspirations were often defined by the immediacy of our surroundings. The size of the world beyond our community was mostly unknown, and as such, our dreams were attached to the reality we experienced daily. When I was a teenager, my ultimate dream wasn't a fancy gadget or an exotic vacation; it was owning a particular breed of donkey.

This wasn't just any donkey; it was the crème de la crème of the donkey world, the kind that was a sign of luxury and status within our community. Comparable to the latest model of a Ferrari, this donkey was the top of rural prestige. It stood tall, its stride was swift and majestic, and it had a distinctive walk that set it apart from the rest. Owning such a creature was not about utility or the work it could do; it was a status symbol, a testament to one's standing within the community.

The concept of modern cars, international travel, or expensive possessions was unknown to us. In our corner of the world, where every resource was valued and nothing was taken for granted, the idea of having such luxuries was almost inconceivable. Instead, dreams were simpler, more grounded, and often linked to our daily lives and the environment in which we lived.

I dedicated two of my summers to work in the farms cultivating onions and potatoes, hoping to save enough money for that prestigious breed of donkey. Despite the hard hours of work and tremendous dedication, my meager wages did not live up to the high price of a donkey. That experience, while it sounds disappointing, instilled in me invaluable lessons about perseverance, the harsh realities of life, and the importance of personal dreams, no matter how simple they may be to the outside world.

Growing up in that remote and isolated town in West Darfur, far from the comforts of civilization and technology, made the first half of my life seem like a century in human history. It was like living in a time capsule. I had been a witness and present at many of the town's "firsts": I was there when the first movie played in town. I witnessed the first electric lamp lighting up a room, and I was there when the first landline telephone was installed in our town. I also saw the first asphalt road, the first camera, and the first plastic bag. I was there when the first modern vehicle rolled into town, when the first airplane landed in a nearby field, and many other "firsts." I witnessed the excitement and amazement of the people every time a new thing came up.

At the nursing center in Italy where I volunteered, the elderly residents who were in their 90s, shared stories about the technology and the developments they had witnessed during their lifetimes. I found myself hesitant and shy to mention that many of my experiences in Darfur were the same as theirs from many decades ago.

In my hometown, we awoke not to alarms but to the sunrise, signaling the start of a new busy day filled with tasks and responsibilities. As children our duties ranged from fetching water from far wells, to herding cows, milking, and working on farms under the severe heat of the sub-Sahara. At times, we even helped construct the traditional round grass huts called Tukuls for some of our neighbors. That made us strong, tough, and disciplined. The regular trips to the market, often twice a day, helped develop our haggling and negotiation skills as we bought groceries.

School added its own set of responsibilities. By the first grade, we had to become self-sufficient. We were washing our own clothes by hand and pressing them with traditional charcoal irons. Summer breaks were not leisure but periods of employment, where we worked to save for the next school year's expenses. Such experiences developed in us the values of hard work and self-reliance from an early age.

Our education was basic but seen as essential for a better future. The classrooms were often under large trees or in basic mud-brick buildings without furniture. Our teachers, brutal and authoritarian, believed in strict discipline as a means to ensure our education. They seemed to communicate through whipping and punishments. A common saying our parents would relay to the teachers was "take the flesh and keep the bones," suggesting teachers were allowed to whip us bloody as long as they didn't break a bone. Homework assignments often felt like pitfalls, leading to the inevitable whipping the next day. Play out in the street was strictly forbidden during the school year, neither after school nor on the weekends.

I'll never forget that day when we were heading home from school. I was in the second grade, and my friends and I were happy because the weekend had arrived. One of my friends crafted a soccer ball from his socks and some plastic bags, and we began playing in the street. Suddenly, the most feared teacher in town passed us on his bicycle on his way home. He looked at us without saying a word. That weekend felt very long, and we could not enjoy it, as we all anticipated the punishment awaiting us once school resumed on Sunday.

After the weekend, the teacher gathered us in front of the entire school. He delivered a strong lecture about the importance of rules and the consequences of breaking them, vowing to make an example out of us so that no student would dare defy the rules again. Fear rolled through us; the student beside me pissed himself. The teacher said, "It doesn't matter even if you went number two; today there will be no mercy."

He called four of the biggest students in the 6th grade and asked them to carry the first student like a hammock with his face down and back facing the sky. The four students each grabbed an arm or a leg, and they lifted and pulled the guy with his face still toward the ground. The teacher started the whipping with all his strength, and the student screamed his pleas for mercy. Lashes like rapid fire licked his back, thighs, and butt, while we stood watching and waiting for our fate. We knew we soon would be next, counting and hoping the punishment wouldn't exceed five lashes. One, two, three, four…. When it reached seven, unconsciously I just took off, running as fast as I could. From behind I heard the teacher's voice yelling, "Get him!"

Out of fear, it felt like I was flying rather than running. The path ahead led directly to a wall, and it seemed there was no escape, yet I pressed on. Just a few feet away from the wall, adrenaline pumped in me, and I jumped grabbing the top of the wall to pull myself over to the other side. As I continued running, I heard other students chasing closely behind. Panic set in. "What should I do? What should I do?" If the students chasing me caught up, I'd receive extra lashes. If I headed home, my father would eventually find out, leading to a whipping there and another back at school. Two rounds of whipping didn't seem appealing. Ultimately, either choice led to the same consequence. Finally, I came to my senses; I decided to circle back to the school on my terms to face my punishment. But I had to do it without being caught by my peers. I managed to do just that and received my fair share of lashes and screaming.

Despite the responsibilities and demands of our childhood and the fear instilled at school, our lives were filled with joy and memorable moments. The playground wasn't limited to a designated area; instead, it was the vast expanse of nature that surrounded us. The sand dunes, rustling bushes, and expansive savannas became our canvas of adventure. Occasionally, this playground would even extend into the wild, where we would catch glimpses of wildlife. We always maintained a safe distance but remained filled with wonder all the same.

Our isolation from the modern world's distractions made us more resourceful and imaginative. Rather than relying on store-bought toys, we channeled our creativity into crafting our own. From makeshift cars made of tin cans and wire to dolls made from discarded cloth and materials, our innovation knew no bounds. These homemade toys, products of our own ingenuity, brought us just as much, if not more, joy than any mass-produced toy could. It was a testament to our resilience, creativity, and the timeless pleasure of simple play.

In our community, elders were an invaluable resource of wisdom, and as children, we gravitated towards them as our primary educators outside the formal schooling. Every evening, as the sun went down, we would gather around them in rapt attention. The gentle glow of the fire would cast extended shadows, making the setting even more magical.

These sessions were more than just a time for storytelling; they were our bridge to the past. With every tale of our ancestors, we felt a deep connection to our roots, understanding the sacrifices and victories that had shaped our community. The folklore, often sprinkled with elements of magic, bravery, and wisdom, was not just for entertainment. These tales often carried moral lessons, teaching us about virtues like courage, honesty, and resilience.

Moreover, the stories were punctuated with real-life lessons from the elder's personal experiences. These anecdotes provided practical advice on navigating the challenges of life. Whether it was dealing with conflicts, understanding the complexities of relationships, or making difficult choices, their words served as a guiding light.

Over time, these evening sessions became foundational in shaping our worldviews. They helped instill values, beliefs, and a sense of belonging. The stories we heard around those fires became a part of our collective memory, ensuring that the cultural identity and communal history were passed down from one generation to the next, preserving the essence of who we were as a people.

Growing up in our town, the ancient African proverb "It takes a village to raise a child" was more than just a saying. It was our lived reality. Our parents undoubtedly played a crucial role in providing for our basic needs and ensuring our wellbeing, but our upbringing was a collective responsibility that extended to the broader community. In essence, we were all products of the rich tapestry of values, lessons, and experiences that the local society provided.

Every person on our street, whether they were directly related to us or not, had a role in our upbringing. They could assign tasks, instill values, and even discipline us if they felt it was necessary. This wasn't seen as an intrusion but rather a reflection of the community's close-knit nature. If an elder saw us misbehaving, they wouldn't hesitate to correct our actions, knowing that this shared responsibility was integral to the fabric of our society. It was this collective guardianship that ensured we grew up with a strong sense of community, understanding our roles within it and the importance of mutual respect and cooperation.

Raising children collectively in a community has numerous positive effects. In my experience, it fosters strong community bonds, ensuring consistent values and enhanced safety for children. Such an upbringing offers diverse learning experiences and shared child-rearing responsibilities, thus promoting resilience in children. The community-driven approach also encourages accountability, reduces feelings of isolation, instills the importance of service, and provides varied avenues for emotional support. In essence, children grow up to be responsible, compassionate, and community minded.

****

A soft knock interrupts my thoughts, and, as the door opens, a hospital worker enters, a tray of dinner in her hands. "Six hours" I muse silently, amazed at how long I've been reflecting on my childhood and life back home.

As I begin to eat, my thoughts take another turn. I start to think about the friends and colleagues I've met in this so-called "first world." There is a clear contrast between our childhoods. I grew up in the so-called "third world." While it might seem judgmental, I can't help but perceive my new friends as emotionally vulnerable, perhaps even a bit spoiled, sensitive, self-centered, and superficial. They appear to me as individuals who often act on whims, driven largely by feelings and sentiments.

The paradox is clear—they grew up in a world of plenty. Even what they call "poverty" is rich by our standards back home. Yet, many of them don't seem to recognize the potential or the opportunities around them. Instead, their lives seem filled with petty complaints and decisions based on feelings and emotions. "I feel like doing this, but I don't feel like doing that." "The weather's making me upset and depressed," and "I'm not in the mood." Such statements are inconceivable to me. I learned from my earliest days that our decisions are often made out of necessity and reason, not preference.

Many of my friends and colleagues' perspectives on discipline, resilience, self-reliance, creativity, and passion seem to revolve around relatively privileged activities and challenges. Their idea of discipline and resilience seems to be nothing more than working hard at a gym to develop a six-pack, flying to Thailand for a two weeklong yoga and healthy diet retreat, traveling to Nepal to climb the K2 summit, or hiking El Camino del Norte in Spain. These activities, while commendable, are pursued as the personal goals of privilege rather than as necessities. Self-reliance and independence might mean nothing more than moving out of a parent's home and getting a job. Yet some of these individuals are unable to even wash their own t-shirts if the washing machine was broken. Creativity and passion seem to be linked to the arts, music, or sports. While I recognize that the values and pursuits of my friends and colleagues are shaped by their unique culture and life circumstances, still their passions often seem superficial to me given my personal experiences and background.

Reflecting upon this, I think about the strength and resilience I, along with other Sudanese, developed growing up. We faced challenges head-on. Our upbringing-built character, discipline, and pragmatism. If only we could merge these values with the resources and opportunities present here, the results would be extraordinary. With our drive and the resources available in this "civilized world," there would be nothing stopping us. It isn't about superiority; it's about recognizing potential, identifying opportunities, and making the most of them.

ASSIM SALIH

CHAPTER 11

Between Life and Legacy

It is December 1st, 2016, a Thursday. Eleven weeks have passed since my first diagnosis by the doctor in Erbil, the one who predicted I had only two or three months to live, a prognosis that was confirmed by multiple other doctors. This suggests that now my remaining time could be just a couple of weeks.

The illness has exhausted my body and weakened me physically. Each step down the hospital corridors is a hard effort, and even the simple joys of playing with my children during their visits have become a challenge. Yet, in their presence, I try to stay strong, attempting to shield them from the full extent of my fragility. Psychologically, I have a heavy mixture of feelings and emotions—there's acceptance of my current state and anticipation of the unknown. Lots of fear and curiosity—a fear of what death feels like, and a curiosity about what comes after death. Each morning gives me gratitude for another day to live, and each night I wonder if it is the last I will ever have.

ECHOES OF FATE

As the clock ticks, I find myself diving in a sea of memories, reflecting upon the countless experiences that have shaped my life. Each moment of joy, every experience of loss, all the lessons learned, and all the achievements won play out in my mind like a movie. Yet, within these reflections, I often catch myself passing judgments on others. It's a complicated emotion. Perhaps it's jealousy, knowing others might have more time than I do. Or perhaps it's sadness, realizing that others don't see the obvious nature of life. I wish they could see, as I now do, that life is too short and that it's essential to prioritize what truly matters, to treasure every moment, and to focus on the genuine essence of existence.

Being in a hospital for days, despite any signs of recovery, can often lead to an inexplicable feeling of illness. The sterile environment, the rhythmic beeping of machines, and the sense of confinement make it hard to envision life outside these walls. The ambiance, the routines, even the scent of antiseptics—everything seems to emphasize illness rather than recovery. This phenomenon sparks a thought: what if a perfectly healthy individual were admitted into such an environment? I hypothesize that just being in such a setting, even without any actual illness, would have a profound psychological impact. Over time, the individual might start to feel genuinely unwell, internalizing the surroundings' emphasis on illness. The longer the stay, the more pronounced this feeling could become, emphasizing the power of environment and perception on our overall wellbeing.

I completely forget about Dr. Andrzej and the experimental surgery that could potentially offer me another shot at life until he knocks on my door and enters with that trademark smile of his. My spirits instantly lift upon seeing him. He asks about my wellbeing and if I'm receiving good care. "Listen," he starts, "you're showing remarkable improvement compared to when you first arrived here a few days ago." His words boost my spirits even more. "I've spoken with the other doctors, and they think you are strong enough to go home and rest for two or three weeks before the surgery." I can't hide my happiness and eagerness to leave, even though they're treating me so well and I have a nice room.

A few jokes and laughter later, Dr. Andrzej gets serious. "Let's focus on the main issue," he begins. "If you're still on board with my procedure, we can schedule the surgery for December 27th. That way, you can spend Christmas with your family." His words fill me with hope. I didn't dare to believe I'd live long enough to see the end of the month and witness another Christmas, but if he's suggesting a date after Christmas, maybe I have a shot. "Now," he continued, "your heart condition is extreme. This procedure isn't guaranteed. As you already know, there is only a 50% chance you'll come out of it alive. I promise to give it my best, but you need to clearly understand the risks."

I reply, a hint of sarcasm in my tone, "Do I have a better alternative?"

He answers straightforwardly, "No, you don't."

I reply with determination. "Given the circumstances, I'm willing to take that risk. So, let's do it."

He dives deep into the specifics of the surgery, detailing which parts they'll replace with mechanical components, the type of tissue needed to patch the heart wall, and many medical terms I can't quite understand. I nod along, pretend understanding, but honestly, I couldn't care less about the technicalities. I just want to see the other side of this bottleneck, whatever that may look like.

He eventually moves on to logistics. "I've coordinated everything with Medicover. My personal team will handle the surgery and the recovery; I want to ensure it's done right, both during and after the procedure." Pausing for a breath, he drops the unexpected good news. "From your end, you'll need to cover Medicover's expenses, which is around $15,000 USD." My jaw nearly hits the floor. Misinterpreting my shock as financial distress, he rushes to explain, "That fee covers the operation theatre, pre-surgery preparations, equipment, ICU, and so forth. My team and I have put our heart and soul into this, we're not seeking payment; success is all the reward we need."

I quickly interrupt him, "Oh, no, Dr. Andrzej. It's not the amount that surprised me. In fact, I was expecting a lot more. For the heart transplant, they quoted me over half a million dollars! So, when you mentioned $15,000, it's like a drop in the ocean compared to that. Trust me, the insurance company will be practically dancing with joy, given the alternative costs. And honestly, if I must, I'll pay that bill myself."

Dr. Andrzej's eyes widened; clearly he was not expecting that response, and then he laughs. "Well, it's not often that a patient is relieved to hear a five-figure medical bill," he remarks with a big smile.

Dr. Andrzej then rises from his chair with a thoughtful look on his face. "Remember," he says, "if there's any new developments, please contact me at any time, and if I have any information we need to discuss, I'll be sure to call you. Otherwise, we'll meet after Christmas."

I nod, appreciating his straightforwardness. "I hope our next meeting is filled with better news," I remark with a hopeful smile.

Dr. Andrzej laughs. "Indeed. Take care and have a wonderful Christmas with your family." With a final nod, he exits the room, leaving me with a mix of hope, anticipation, and gratitude.

****

The soft sound of raindrops wakes me up. Outside the hospital window, the world is covered in gray shadows, the day is soaked in rain. However, for me, this morning is full of promises. My time in the hospital, which in reality only lasted a few days, seemed to me to have stretched into a few months. My spirits are lifted not only because I am about to leave this place but also because of the beacon of hope that Dr. Andrzej installed in me during his visit yesterday evening. It offered a possibility—one that could allow me to celebrate another Christmas with those I hold dearest and perhaps give me more moments afterwards. In my circumstances, every additional minute is invaluable. The surgery, which has only a 50% success rate, still fills me with optimism, confident that it will pave the way for many more years to witness my children flourish and offer me a new chapter to embrace life again.

Nurses come in and leave. The room is being cleaned by one of the hospital staff, breakfast is being served, and it's still early for the discharge time. So, I open my laptop to pass some time, and the first email is from Olena asking about my wellbeing, where I am on this planet, and hoping my family is all right. What a lovely surprise.

In April 2011, I was sent along with several others to Zambia to combat a deadly measles outbreak that had spread among the locals in the Northern part of Zambia. We were based in Kasama, a small town in the northern province. It had been a challenging mission; we had to vaccinate over a million individuals located in remote small villages in the bushes and jungles of deepest Africa. There had been no road access to most of the villages, we had faced numerous wildlife hazards and risks, and the rainfall was continuous. We had worked around 18 hours a day without weekends, vacations, or breaks for months.

During the mission, I developed a bad toothache, but I didn't have the time to seek out a dentist. The owner of the hotel where we stayed, Mr. King, informed me there was only one dentist in the city. She was a good friend of his, and he assured me she wouldn't mind if he asked her to come by and check on me. Sure enough, the following day she arrived. To my surprise, she was tall, with white skin and blonde hair, clearly not a local from Kasama. While there were many white individuals in Zambia, most resided in the capital due to the better internet connection, consistent electricity, air conditioning, and more comfortable lifestyle.

Mr. King introduced me to her, explaining that Olena was a Ukrainian dentist. She had been in Kasama for over a decade, volunteering and serving the people in and around the town. This was particularly noteworthy because native dentists often refused to live and settle in such a remote area.

I have always held the idea that we humanitarian workers are noble. Our daily tasks revolved around serving people who were suffering, providing dignity, and saving their lives. Although our intentions were pure, we still received salaries, enjoyed benefits, and took vacations, which somehow mitigated the impact of our sacrifices. Then I met Olena. Here was a woman who embodied the essence of selflessness and sacrifice. For more than a decade, she had volunteered tirelessly in one of the most challenging environments in the world, without the comforts and guarantees that come with a regular job. Her dedication was not based on the paycheck at the end of the month but on the smiles of those she helped. It made me reflect on the depth of our commitments and the true nature of service.

In today's complex world, humanitarian action offers the hope of a future, embodying compassion, resilience, and a commitment to alleviating the suffering of the vulnerable. However, as with any profession, individuals enter the field with a range of motivations—some are sincerely driven to assist, while others may have different priorities.

Many individuals, especially from Europe and America, where job competition can be tense and even the best of qualifications might not land a good job, turn to the humanitarian sector for employment. International Non-Governmental Organizations (INGOs), particularly those based in the U.S., offer generous benefits, often matching or exceeding what they can hope to get in their home countries. For some, it is the prestige, power, and authority that come with the role that is most attractive, not a genuine desire to make a difference. Others see it as an opportunity to boost their resume, are more thrilled by the prospect of free travel and adventure than committed to the actual mission or see it as a journey of personal discovery and development.

On the other hand, individuals from developing countries in Africa, the Middle East, and Asia, particularly those accustomed to living through humanitarian crises, bring a unique perspective to their responsibilities. Although they often face challenges due to their passport and visa restrictions, their backgrounds and first-hand experiences from their home countries make them invaluable in the field. But honestly, many of these individuals are driven by the benefits and salary offered by INGOs, which can be significantly higher than those afforded to the upper classes in their home countries.

Throughout my journey in this sector, I have encountered many individuals whose basic intentions were not truly aligned with the humanitarian mission. Unfortunately, they often make up a large percentage of the humanitarian workforce. It is easy to spot them in challenging operational situations through their actions, behaviors, and their lack of passion and compassion towards the very communities they are supposed to serve. They often prioritize safeguarding their own positions and wellbeing over addressing the needs of the beneficiaries they serve.

Personally, I must admit, my entry into the humanitarian world was somewhat accidental. I found myself a refugee and homeless in Italy. The streets of Milan and the train stations were my home. I was in desperate search for a job and a new beginning. Despite my solid background in air operations management and information technology, securing a job was challenging. I applied for numerous positions, including office cleaner and housemaid, yet not a single interview came my way.

That is when I crossed paths with Alessandro, an extraordinary young man from the small northeastern Italian town of Rovereto. Unlike other Italians, Alessandro opened not just his heart and home to me for a meal, a shower, or sometimes a place to spend the night. He assisted with translations and helped me to better understand Italian culture. Importantly, he provided me with access to a computer and the internet, enhancing my ability to find opportunities and jobs. When Alessandro noticed my struggle with job-hunting, he suggested I remove my photo from the resume. To my astonishment, interview invitations began filling my inbox. However, the moment I appeared for these interviews, and they noticed the color of my skin, I was often dismissed before the conversation even began.

After a few "interviews" where I experienced rejection based on my skin color, I realized that searching for work in Italy would be pointless. I shifted my focus towards international opportunities. During this hunt, I came across a job opportunity with a Swiss INGO named Medair. The term "air" caught my eye, and immediately I applied without understanding what an INGO stood for. A few days later, Medair reached out, detailing the position, its requirements, and their values. They expected me to cover half of the airfare to Afghanistan, where the job was located. I thought, "If I had money to pay for half of the airfare, I'd surely be having a nice dinner, and sleeping in a cozy bed, not on a luxurious park bench!" Consequently, I decided not to continue with Medair's recruitment process.

Nevertheless, the same website where I discovered the Medair's opportunity was rich with resources and job openings from various other INGOs. Subsequently, I spent dozens of hours learning about the humanitarian sector and exploring job opportunities. Then I found a job opening with another INGO. And, in a blink of an eye, my life transitioned from the rough street style to flying across the world. I was assigned to Indonesia for the 2004 Tsunami emergency as my first humanitarian mission. Upon arrival, I was given $100 USD for emergency use, to cover urgent purchases in scenarios where I might not have enough cash, where ATMs were not functioning, or where

I found myself in similar situations. Instead, I immediately bought a couple of shirts, jeans, and pair of shoes to look presentable.

On my first day at work, I came to truly understand the essence of INGOs and the profound impact of humanitarian work. I couldn't help but see a reflection of my own people from Darfur in the faces of those suffering from manmade or natural disasters. Their pain mirrored my recent experiences—the hopelessness, homelessness, joblessness, and difficulties that I was living just days prior to starting that mission. Their struggles were the same as mine, and their desperation for survival paralleled my own. In working to assist them, I felt like I was helping a former version of myself, and, in a larger sense, helping my people back in Darfur.

This personal connection with the vulnerable and the suffering fueled the passion and dedication in my humanitarian journey. Every day, my commitment to the cause deepened. Along the way, I encountered my fair share of disagreements with colleagues and higher-ups who seemed detached from the very essence of our mission. I often found myself disagreeing with how certain organizations poorly executed their programs or failed to really live out their purported values. While I have always strived for career growth and fair compensation, my primary motivation always remained unchanged. My loyalty and devotion were never to a particular organization or superior but only to the vulnerable people and those in dire need. I was always ready to go the extra mile for them, even if it meant putting myself at risk.

Yet, despite all my experiences and convictions, I couldn't help but feel humbled and ashamed when I met Olena in Zambia. Learning about her years of dedicated volunteer work and her unwavering commitment to the humanitarian cause put things into deep perspective for me, and I was honored to meet such an amazing person. Since that time, we maintained contact, exchanging emails every few months to check on each other's wellbeing.

****

Immediately after finishing my lunch, the head of the cardiology department at Medicover Hospital came in to personally oversee my discharge process. He hands me some medications to last until my next meeting with Dr. Andrzej, and I make my way to my beloved ones.

Being outside the hospital after facing a life-threatening situation is an intensely emotional experience. The sterile, often impersonal environment of the hospital, with its constant monitoring and uncertainty, can make the freedom of being discharged feel like a rebirth. I'm overwhelmed with relief and gratitude for life itself and for the dedicated medical professionals who looked after me. Underlying these positive feelings, however, are feelings of vulnerability, fear about the journey ahead, and worry about what will happen after Christmas.

On my way home, I make a stop to see my older son, who is staying at a hotel with his mom. As the taxi nears Inflancka street, I ask the driver to pull over a couple of blocks short. I want to walk a bit, to breathe some fresh air, and enjoy the freedom. At the hotel, my son is visibly happy to see me; still, I detect hints of worry and sadness on his face. To reassure him, I talk about my strength and assure him that everything will be okay. His mother had bought him a chess set, so we spend a couple of hours engaging in conversation, playing, and teaching him some chess moves. Once home, I spend the rest of the day with my wife and younger son.

While having dinner, my phone rings. I decide to ignore it and continue eating. A couple of minutes later, it rings again. Thinking, "Maybe it's something important," I get up to answer it. Dr. Andrzej's name flashes on the screen. "Good evening, Doctor. How are you?" I ask.

"Well, I'm all right, but I'm worried about you," he replies.

Touched by his concern, I respond, "I'm doing fine, made it home safely, and now I'm enjoying time with my family."

He falls silent for a few seconds, then speaks to someone with him in Polish. I recognize the voice of the other person; it's the head of the cardiology department at Medicover Hospital. I stay silent until he finishes his conversation. "Listen," he begins, "I'm reviewing your medical records from last week during your stay at the hospital. I'm sorry, but you might not make it until Christmas."

At that moment, I feel like someone has suddenly splashed me with ice water. I'm paralyzed, overwhelmed by anxiety and fear. My breathing becomes rapid, and my heart races so fast that it feels like it wants to break out of my chest and run away.

The news doesn't shock me; I'm aware of my condition and have braced myself for the worst. However, what truly worries me is the hesitation and concern I detect in Dr. Andrzej's voice, which he's never shown before. His voice sounds hopeless and unsure, which is so unlike him. My entire future if I have one, depends on him, and now I feel he's wavering.

Suddenly, his voice brings me back. "Hello, hello, Assim, are you still there?"

I reply, "Yes, I'm listening."

He continues, "I want you to enjoy tomorrow, Saturday, with your family, but you need to check-in on Sunday, no later than noon. We must do the surgery first thing Monday morning." He takes a deep breath and continues, "Until then, please go easy on yourself, no strenuous efforts of any kind, meanwhile I'll gather my team and have them ready. Does that sound Ok?"

I simply reply, "Yes."

He concludes, "All right then, see you Sunday afternoon at the hospital. Good night."

After he hangs up, I try to keep calm, taking a couple of deep breaths. I give Ali a quick call to let him know what is going on, then return to finish my dinner as if nothing has happened. I relay the news to my wife, assuring her everything is fine and that when I wake up next week, I'll start a new life.

****

Today is Sunday, December 4, 2016, at precisely 8:11 in the evening. Since my last phone conversation with Dr. Andrzej two days ago, I barely have enough energy or clarity to write down my thoughts. I have weird feelings, almost as if I'm floating outside of myself. It is like my soul has already left my body. I am trying my best to be normal and continue as usual. As best I could, I spent yesterday playing with my kids and chatting with my ex and my wife. Even though I was pretending like nothing serious was happening, in reality, I felt dead.

I have been through many surgeries and overcome various challenges in my life. Historically, I've faced them with confidence and optimism, always believing I'd recover and return to my life. Yet, this time feels distinctly different. As I write this, worries and fears weigh heavily on my mind, grappling with the reality of my mortality. I'm struggling to come to terms with the fact that I may not be able to overcome this hurdle. Slowly, I'm attempting to accept my fate and find peace within myself.

While spending time with my family yesterday, I also reached out to the dearest people in my life, including my relatives back home, sharing news of my surgery. I painted it as a simple and straightforward procedure, even though deep down I knew it was my last time to hear their voices. On social media, I wrote a short message "Hello, friends. I'll be undergoing a medical procedure Monday morning. I might be offline for a while, but I'll see you on the other side." I did not want to explain the gravity of the situation, hoping to grant them a joyful weekend before they heard the potentially shocking news of my passing.

I haven't prayed in years, and I won't start now. If God truly exists, He might see my prayers now as hypocritical. But if He does exist, He'll know the intentions behind my actions throughout my life—both the good and the mistakes.

This morning, my wife and younger son accompanied me to the hospital as I checked in. Saying goodbye without truly saying it was heart breaking. Later, my ex and older son came to visit, and those goodbyes were equally difficult. Holding and kissing my children, not wanting to let them go, I felt an overwhelming desire to share with them the lessons I've learned, values I hold dear, and advice on staying true to themselves as they navigate life. But they are too young to fully understand these things, and there simply wasn't enough time. Watching my family leave the hospital, knowing I'd never see them again, tore at my heart. However, I didn't want to burden them with sadness and so I let them go peacefully.

Ali and another Sudanese friend, Idris, dropped by the hospital that evening. We went again through my wishes in detail, discussing the plan of my burial. We revisited the list of contacts, close friends, and relatives who should be the first to hear the news. I felt comforted knowing that Ali and Idris, trusted friends, would handle these final affairs with the care and respect they deserved.

For the past 48 hours, my mind has been occupied with one profound thought: the legacy I wish to leave behind for my sons in the form of a message. This isn't just any message, but one that highlights my life's journey, my love, my hopes, and my dreams for them. A message that helps them to navigate their lives, guiding them during moments of doubt and offering solace for those times when they miss having me beside them. As I sit here, writing, surrounded by the sterile environment of the hospital, I am trying to capture all my feelings and all what I wish for them. Here is what I write:

ECHOES OF FATE

My dearest sons,

I wish I could sit down with you both and share these words, these feelings, these lessons face-to-face, savoring each moment together. But life, in its unpredictable ways, forced me to write them down instead.

I wrote this book to document the lives of those who have influenced me deeply—individuals whose essence I find in every step I take. It is important for you to understand their values and the qualities that made them so special to me. While some of them have passed on to the next world and may have faded in the memories of others, I tried to bring them alive on these pages so that you may draw wisdom from them.

I detailed the legacy of your great-grandfather, a man respected and loved by anyone lucky enough to cross his path, for his unwavering morals, principles, and honesty. I shed light on the life of your grandmother, perhaps the most resilient person I've ever known. Despite her life full of hardships and challenges, she never gave up. Her resilience was not for herself but to pave a brighter path for her daughters.

This book also captures the fleeting and touching life of my childhood friend, Sabir. A soul who, despite being deprived of life's basic joys through an extreme childhood, never stopped smiling in the face of his challenges; his courage exceeded the greatest warriors. His journey was cut short, but his brief lifetime illuminated mine.

I wrote of the touching love story between Giuseppe and Mariana. Their story is a testament to the power of love. Even after life separated them for decades, fate brought them together in their later years. They took the opportunity to relive a romance they never had the chance to fully explore and remained inseparable until the very end.

I wrote this book to motivate you to think deeply about the true essence of existence, to instill in you the correct views on life and values, and to protect you from the superficiality that so often pollutes so many in today's world. Through these pages, I aimed to provide clarity on one's purpose in life and provide insights that may save you years of searching and potential regret. Contrary to my earlier belief that the only purpose of life is the pursuit of happiness, I have come to realize that such a pursuit, while comforting, is also somewhat limiting. Instead, your true calling is to be of service to yourself, to those around you, and to contribute, in any capacity you can, to the progress of humanity. Your purpose isn't just about defining who you want to be but understanding and recognizing the role you play in the lives of others.

A wise man once said, "If you visit a cemetery and observe the headstones, you'll find the essence of life's purpose." Each headstone often reads "BELOVED FATHER," "CHERISHED MOTHER," "DEAR SISTER" and so on, or it might mention a notable role like "DEVOTED TEACHER." Yet, these headstones never describe an individual's personal feelings, whether contentment, happiness, or any other introspective sentiment.

I wrote this book to highlight the privileges you have, being born in a part of the world full of opportunities that many can only dream of. I wish you to appreciate and take advantage of these opportunities and use them to shape your own destiny. You have the potential to excel in any path you choose, especially if you embody the resilience and perseverance of your great grandmother Hawa, and if you adhere to the morals and values of your grandfather Mohammed. If you embrace the unwavering vision, patience, and positivity of my friend Sabir, and if you treasure love as deeply and passionately as Giuseppe and Mariana did.

ECHOES OF FATE

My sons, life will introduce you to a diverse range of people. Some will be genuine, providing comfort to your soul—treasure them. Yet, you'll also meet those who might appear as good friends or lovers but ultimately betray and hurt you, like my experience with Orderud. When faced with betrayal, aim to rise above, avoid pondering the reasons or seeking revenge. Instead, choose the path of understanding and compassion, letting go of the hurt. It is hard, but always be the better person, ensuring your heart remains open and forgiving even when confronted with dishonesty and deception.

I wrote this book to deliver a crucial bit of advice: never walk blindly on anyone else's path, especially when it comes to deep personal matters such as religion, politics, or love. You are fortunate to live in a world that favors inquiry, where open discussion, debate, and critical thinking are not only accepted but also celebrated. It is necessary to dive deep, explore different perspectives, and challenge the pre-existing notions. Only then can you make informed decisions. Whatever conclusions you reach, it is important that they come from a place of deep reflection and true understanding, not just imitation. Your beliefs and convictions should be yours alone, shaped by careful thought and personal experience.

My dear sons, I hoped to be by your side through every twist and turn of life. I dreamed of cheering you on during your favorite sports matches, seeing you grow year after year, and celebrating every birthday with joy. The thought of accompanying you to your schools for career days, of sharing our summer adventures, and of cheering your graduation filled my heart with warmth. I hoped to celebrate your first paycheck, to support you as you raise a family, to hold my grandchildren just as I once carried you, and perhaps even to walk them through the parks as we used to do. More than anything else, I wanted to be not only your father but also your best friend, sharing happy moments and revealing my true self to you. I wanted to be there with you for a long time, but destiny decided otherwise. While my physical presence may fade away, always remember that I will watch over you from above, forever beside you in spirit. Regrettably, I'm still uncertain about the afterlife, but if there's a heaven, I hope to see you there.

My dear sons, my love for you is eternal. Goodbye for now.

THE END

ECHOES OF FATE

Afterword

As we reach the end of 'Echoes of Fate: From Birth to the Last Heartbeats,' I am acutely aware that this narrative may have stirred many questions and reflections. What were the results of my surgery? Did it bring the hope and healing I anticipated? Indeed, what primarily led to my heart condition, and how have I grappled with its life-altering implications? These and other questions hint at the deeper layers of my journey not yet fully explored in this volume.

While I have touched on various aspects of my life and hinted at many mysteries, I realize that I've provided more questions than answers. How did I transition from the arid landscapes of Darfur to pivotal roles on the global stage? How did I end up navigating the complexities of air operations management and landmine clearance? What series of events led to my becoming a refugee and living homeless in Europe? The pathways which lead to the answers for these questions are as intricate as they are fascinating, filled with challenges and lessons that have shaped my existence. Each step, each decision, is part of a larger story yet to be fully told.

For now, I must leave some of these lines of enquiry unanswered, keeping further revelations for future stories where you can discover how my journey continues. However, I am eager to share one crucial piece of information. I successfully cheated death once again, thanks to Dr. Andrzej's clinical trial. This groundbreaking endeavor gave me a renewed lease of life—a chance not only to witness my children's growth into the unique selves but has led to exciting new life adventures and experiences. This gift of time has deepened my commitment to assisting the marginalized and vulnerable, allowing me to continue repaying my debt to a world that has given me so much. It is another opportunity to be more grateful and thankful.

As you reflect on the pages of this book, I hope you carry with you not just the facts of a life lived across continents and crises, but also the spirit of perseverance and a dose of the hope that has driven me. I also hope that it may inspire you to explore your paths (new and old), confront your challenges with courage, discover life's true purposes and values, and, above all, make a meaningful, beneficial impact on the world around you.

Thank you for sharing this part of my journey. There is more to come, and I look forward to discovering where our paths will intersect next. Until then, let us each strive to leave a positive mark on the world, echoing the fate that propels us forward.

— Your companion in reflection and action, Assim

UPCOMING RELEASE: LOST BETWEEN TWO SKIES

I'm thrilled to share with you my next literary journey, "Lost Between Two Skies," which will be released soon. In this true-inspired fiction, I delve into the mysteries of the celestial realm. Drawing upon the same passion and emotion that fueled the pages of "Echoes of Fate," "Lost Between Two Skies" promises to reshape your perception of life and what lies beyond.

I can't wait for you to join me on this new adventure. Stay tuned for updates on the release date and how you can get your hands on a copy. Thank you for your continued support and enthusiasm!

For new releases and updates subscribe at:

www.AssimSalih.com

ABOUT THE AUTHOR

Assim Salih's life is a journey across continents, from his beginnings in Darfur to his impactful work as a global humanitarian, has deeply influenced his literary creations. His literary voice, enriched by diverse cultural experiences, weaves a tapestry of human stories. His writings, a blend of cultural insights and human celebration, delve deep into the human condition. Filled with empathy and philosophical depth, Assim's narratives encourage readers to appreciate global diversity and shared human experiences. His work is not just storytelling; it's a journey through life's complexities, offering valuable perspectives and insights on every page.

www.AssimSalih.com

Printed in the USA
CPSIA information can be obtained
at www.ICGtesting.com
LVHW050239010624
781580LV00001B/46